EVOLUTION MYTHS

EVOLUTION MYTHS
A Critical View of neo-Darwinism

Jeffrey K. Lyons

Liberty Hill Publishing

Liberty Hill Publishing
2301 Lucien Way #415
Maitland, FL 32751
407.339.4217
www.LibertyHillPublishing.com

Includes biblographical references and index.
1. Charles Darwin 2. Evolution 3. Origin of Life 4. Dinosaurs
5. Bacteria 6. DNA – Francis Crick 7. Philosophy – Mind 8. Scientific
Method – Francis Bacon 9. Cave Paintings – Altamira

Library of Congress Control: 2018963244

Printed in the United States of America.

ISBN-13: 978-1-54564-818-6

*To all those students, researchers, and lifetime learners
who remain courageous enough to ask questions
that dare challenge ideological barriers,
may you remain intellectually honest in your
pursuit of knowledge and to my son Stephen.*

Contents

Table of Figures

Acknowledgements

To my dear wife, Elizabeth who has endured this project for over seven years and has provided both feedback and proofreading input. Special thanks for Dr. Ralph Kam for his input on the text and feedback. Thank you to my son Daniel who has provided feedback and comments which have been addressed in the text. Special thanks to my publishers for their insightful suggestions regarding improvements to the text and future companion publications.

Introduction

*Reverence for natural truth and the deep, earliest,
scientific methods of searching after it are what is taught
here; so that we who have passed beyond these doors are
gladly welcomed among that resolute band of nature-
workers who both propel and guide the great plowshare
of science on through the virgin sod of the unknown.*
Geologist Clarence King (1842-1901)[1]

*. . . dissent and contradiction have been a fixture of
scientific dialogue - and have certainly fertilized it.*
**Professor of Mineralogy and Petrography,
Wolf Uwe Reimold** [2]

I have always wanted to write a book that critically examines
the term evolution. I am not a biologist. I have a PhD in
Communication. I have taught on the university level for close to 10
years at different state and private universities. One thing that I have
always stressed with my students is that to have a conversation, we
need to first define the terms.

The term *evolution* means a lot of things to different people.
According to the National Academy of Sciences: "Biological

---

[1]   Speaking to the Sheffield Scientific School at Yale College (1877, p. 449). King
      was the founding member of the US Geological Survey, established in 1879.
[2]   (Reimold, 2007)

evolution refers to changes in the traits of organisms over multiple generations" (National Academy of Sciences and Institute of Medicine., 2008, p. 4).

We will examine this definition of evolution (and others) in more detail in this book. The point is, most of us are familiar with the term evolution, and yet few of us have critically examined what is meant by the word – or how it has affected our society. That is why I have written this book; it is meant as a guide and a springboard for discussion and critical thinking.

My approach in writing this book is to examine the writings and research of those scientists, biologists, and philosophers who have been influential in the advancement of evolutionary thinking. Most sources quoted in this book are advocates of evolutionary theory. What are they saying to us today? How does this affect our lives? Do their arguments and ideas have merit?

This book is written for, the college student, the bewildered parent and anyone who has ever been interested in how the term *evolution* became so influential in our society today. This book is not written for the scientific community; however, I would not be surprised if members of the academy choose to respond to the contents of this work.[3] It is my goal to touch on many of foundational cornerstones of evolutionary theory and offer a critical evaluation of the premises upon which they are built.

As a former university professor, I always encouraged my students to think critically. The development of critical thinking skills should be a primary objective of higher education. The inclusion of critical thinking into the mission statements and department objectives of many higher education institutions is not uncommon. If I would advance the notion that *evolutionary theory* is flawed and needs a major overhaul, to the point of possible replacement with a more adequate theory. Such an idea would be considered academic heresy at most secular universities.

---

[3]   The author welcomes intellectually honest feedback on the topics in this work. No work is a perfect one. It is my hope that future editions of this initial work will offer additional refinement and expansion of these topics.

Does Quantity of Research Justify the Premise?

There are those who would respond that evolution is no longer a theory; it is a scientific fact. I quote those scientists who advance this argument; I credit them for their boldness. They assert that so much has been published on the topic of evolution that it has tipped the scales from scientific theory to established fact. They will say that there are millions of pages of published research. Therefore, the theory must be true. This is clearly a fallacious argument.

Quantity of published research does not establish scientific fact. Rather, it is compelling arguments that establish scientific principles. Isaac Newton demonstrated this with his *Mathematical Principles of Natural Philosophy* (1687/1803). Newton's work was so revolutionary, that it changed the entire western scientific understanding of physics, gravity, and optics. One man's work changed the entire course of scientific understanding. Thousands of pages of research and hundreds of books and studies by hundreds of scientists was not necessary.

Microbiologist Michael Behe (1998) points out that Galen, a physician in Rome in the second century, proposed the idea that blood was pumped in a one-way direction out of the heart to the body. This theory necessitated the notion that new blood was therefore being continuously made in the body. Doctors and medical professionals accepted this theory as fact for centuries until it was challenged by Willian Harvey.

William Harvey in the seventeenth century disproved Galen. As Behe (1998) puts it, "Harvey calculated that if the heart pumps out just two ounces of blood per beat, at 72 beats per minute, in one hour it would have pumped 540 pounds of blood – triple the weight of a man! (p. 8). Harvey used critical thinking and mathematical computation to disprove Galen's theory. Ironically, it took 15 centuries for Harvey to disprove Galen! It only took one man's critical thinking, to alter 15 centuries of established scientific understanding theory of human blood flow and the circulatory system. It is a fallacious argument to suggest that volumes of research and longevity of consensus establishes a scientific fact. Scientific knowledge and conclusions can be challenged at any time; indeed, they can be overturned if new evidence, research and critical thinking support a sounder theory. This is precisely what philosopher of science, Thomas Kuhn (1962/1996) referred to when he documented that many similar scientific revolutions have been taking place for centuries. Kuhn's seminal work is considered one of the greatest scientific books of the 20th century, *The Structure of Scientific Revolutions*. The book is not an easy read, but it is essential to understanding how scientific theories are created, accepted, refuted, revised, debated and distributed throughout academia. The fact is scientific theories are human creations, they are representations of the natural world. As human creations, scientific theories are always open to revision, fine-tuning, replacement and modification.

Scientific Theories Are Not Sacrosanct [4]

Scientific discovery is a heuristic process; discovery begins at some point of uncertainty and then advances toward the known. The problem is that the current state of evolutionary theory (or the application of neo-Darwinism) is that it comes from a place of scientific dogma with almost ubiquitous application.

Geologist Donald Prothero (2007a) rightly observed that, "it is not a good thing when a field in science seems to have all the answers and is no longer questioning its assumptions" (p. 94). This book is intended to challenge many of the assumptions of evolutionary theory and neo-Darwinism.

To challenge Darwin is tantamount to career suicide for the modern biologist. Predictably, many scientists and philosophers that are challenging Darwin are from fields of scientific enquiry outside of biology. These are not religious zealots with an ax to grind. These are intellectually honest researchers who are courageous enough to challenge the existing evolutionary paradigm. In this book, you will meet many researchers that are bravely challenging the current orthodoxy of evolution. One such voice is Dr. Jeremy Narby, (1998)

---

[4]   *Sacrosanct* - Sacred and beyond criticism or change. The history of science is one of future discovery, revision and change (Kuhn, 1962/1996).

an anthropologist who concludes the following in his book, *The Cosmic Serpent: DNA and the Origins of Knowledge*:

> I do not intend to attack anybody's faith, but to demarcate the blind spot of the rational and fragmented gaze of contemporary biology and to explain why my hypothesis is condemned in advance to remain in that spot. To sum up: My hypothesis is based on the idea that DNA in particular and nature in general are minded. This contravenes the founding principle of molecular biology that is the current orthodoxy. (p. 145)

This book seeks to address the neo-Darwinian blind spot, that anthropologist Dr. Jeremy Narby refers to.

Why I Wrote This Book

Colleagues have asked me: What gives you the right to criticize evolutionary theory? After all, they say, I have neither a background in biology or the physical sciences. My response is straightforward. Evolution ceased to be a biological theory a long time ago. It is a metatheory, or put simply, a theory of theories. Today, evolution is imbedded in the following literature (and more): biology, geology, paleontology, systematics, genetics, population genetics, astronomy, anthropology, sociology, psychology, ethics and my field of communication. Ironically, there are frequent gaps of empirical evidence in the field of biological evolution. Where gaps exist, there is a generous use of deductive reasoning and narrative, which is used to glue the story together. Narrative becomes the super glue that fills in holes where empirical evidence is lacking, beginning with biology! Therefore, I have written this book to challenge the paradigm, or what Dr. Jeremy Narby (1998) calls, "the current orthodoxy" (p. 145). Get ready for a ride!

I. Myth 1: Charles Darwin Created a Theory Called *Evolution*

*Evolution has been a contentious idea within
society since it was first articulated by Charles
Darwin and Alfred Russel Wallace in 1858*
National Academy of Sciences [5]

This chapter is a human story. In this chapter, you will read something that you have never been taught in high school in the United States of America (USA). If you grew up in the USA, you were probably taught about evolution, beginning in elementary school. You probably were taught that living things change over time. In high school you probably learned about DNA, mutations, and natural selection. You learned about Darwin and his trip to the Galapagos Islands and that it was Darwin that created a theory called evolution. In this chapter, you will discover that Darwin did not create a theory called evolution and that there was a philosopher named Herbert Spencer who coined the term *evolution* and changed Darwin's original theory. As we shall see, science does not occur in a vacuum. It is created by humans and it is important to understand the historical development of the ideas that influence our thinking.

In this chapter, I intend to discuss the term *evolution* and the development of the theory of evolution. I will demonstrate that

---

[5]   (National Academy of Sciences and Institute of Medicine., 2008, p. 12)

evolution was not a term that Darwin initially introduced when he and Wallace published their joint paper in 1858. *Evolution* was not a term used by Darwin when he published the first edition of *On the Origin of Species*, in 1859. In fact, the term *evolution* did not appear in the first five editions of On the *Origin of Species*! It was not until many years after 1858 that Darwin adopted the term *evolution* and used it to refer to his original theories about the development of life on earth.

At this point some may be asking, "Why does it matter who came up with the term *evolution*?" This is the question that I will be addressing throughout this chapter. It is very important to trace the origin of the term evolution because *evolution* is now a ubiquitous term that is freely applied outside of the field of biology. How did this come about? What were Darwin's initial intentions when proposing his theories? How has evolution impacted Western thinking?

We begin our inquiry by going back to 1858, the year that Wallace and Darwin made their groundbreaking presentation before the Linnean Society in London. Today, the name Darwin is a household name, but who was Wallace and what was his role in relation to Darwin?

Wallace and Darwin

Alfred Russel Wallace (1823 -1913) was a British naturalist who traveled to remote destinations to collect specimens and publish his findings. In 1849, Wallace teamed up with British naturalist Henry Walter Bates for a three-year exploration of the Amazon River basin. During this time, they collected specimens and documented their discoveries. The specimens were brought back to England and sold to universities and museums for their collections. By 1853, Wallace published several scientific articles and two books: *Palm Trees of the Amazon and Their uses* (1853) and *Narrative of Travels on the Amazon and Rio Negro* (1853/1889). As a result, Alfred Russel Wallace gained a reputation as a skilled naturalist and collector of exotic specimens.

In 1854, Wallace received funding for his own expedition, this time to the Malay Archipelago (Indonesia and Malaysia). It was during his trip to Malaysia that Wallace began to formulate his own theory of natural selection, the idea that competition among living things allows beneficial traits to be passed on to future generations – which in turn contributes to the formulation of new species over time.

Wallace was familiar with Darwin who had published his account of his journey aboard the *Beagle* in 1839 as: *Narrative of the surveying voyages of His Majesty's Ships Adventure and Beagle between the years 1826 and 1836.* The younger Wallace, sent a paper to the more established naturalist, Darwin. In that paper, Wallace shared his own theory of natural selection, which was remarkably similar to Darwin's.

When Darwin received Wallace's correspondence in London, Darwin must have been shocked. Darwin could see that Wallace had independently come to the same conclusion regarding the process of natural selection. The somewhat reluctant Darwin had been gathering data and polishing his theory of natural selection for about 20 years without publishing. Darwin surmised that if he did not publish soon, Wallace or someone else would get the credit for his ideas on the origin of species.

The compromise solution was that Charles Darwin and Alfred Wallace published a co-authored paper titled: "On the Tendency of Species to Form Varieties: and on the Perpetuation of Varieties and Species by Natural Means of Selection." The paper was read July 1, 1858, and it was published in the third volume of the *Journal of the Linnean Society* (Darwin & Wallace, 1858). [6]

Darwin and Wallace's paper was certainly groundbreaking. However, now that Darwin's ideas were made public, he needed to publish his more complete work to distinguish himself from Wallace. Therefore, in the following year of 1859, Darwin published his work on which he had labored 20 years: *On the Origin of Species by*

---

[6] The Linnean Society was founded in 1788 and was named after the Swedish naturalist Carl Linnaeus (1707–1778). It is the world's oldest active biological society.

Means of Natural Selection: Or, the Preservation of Favored Races in the Struggle for Life.

The Evolution of the Term *Evolution*

Prior to Darwin, there was nothing particularly remarkable about the word evolution. In his *American Dictionary of the English Language* (1828) Noah Webster defined *evolution* as: "the act of unfolding or unrolling."

This is in stark contrast to what we read today about evolution. Evolutionary biologist, Ernst Mayr writes in his book *What Evolution is* that ". . . Darwin did far more than postulate evolution (and present overwhelming evidence for its occurrence); he also proposed an explanation for evolution that did not rely on any supernatural powers or forces" (Mayr, 2001, p. 9). Professor of Philosophy Michael Ruse, a staunch defender of Darwin writes, ". . . Charles Darwin had published *On the Origin of Species*, where he argued that all organisms are the end result of a long, slow, natural process of development known as evolution" (Ruse, 2004, p. 33). Today, the name of Darwin has become synonymous with the term evolution. We assume that Darwin proposed a theory called evolution which has now become the cornerstone of modern biological science. But what actually happened?

In actuality, Charles Darwin, the author of *On the Origin of Species* never did originally propose a theory called evolution. The word "evolution" is not in the text of the first printing of *The Origin of Species: By means of natural selection or The preservation of favored Races in the struggle for life* (1859). In fact, the word *evolution* is not mentioned until the 6th (and final) edition of *The Origin of Species* (Darwin, 1889)!

What Theory did Darwin Propose?

Darwin proposed a theory called *descent with modification*. He described his theory in the following manner:

On the theory of descent with modification, the great law of the long enduring, but not immutable, succession of the same types within the same areas, is at once explained; for the inhabitants of each quarter of the world will obviously tend to leave in that quarter, during the next succeeding period of time, closely allied though in some degree modified descendants. (1876/1998, pp. 475-476)

Darwin's original proposition was that descent with modification was the result of a process called natural selection. In terms of cause and effect, natural selection was the proposed cause, while descent with modification was the effect. This cause and effect relationship that Darwin proposed can be seen in Darwin's (1876/1998) own words:

. . . the other great leading facts from paleontology agree admirably with the theory of descent with modification through variation and natural selection. We can thus understand how it is that new species come in slowly and successively . . . (p. 479)

This is the scientific method that Darwin referred to in his autobiography when he stated, "I worked on Baconian[7] principles . . ." (Barlow, 2005, p. 98). Prior to Darwin, the prevailing scientific explanation for life on earth was one of special creation. Darwin introduced a new force into the equation, natural selection as an explanation. We will talk about natural selection in more detail in the next chapter.

One truly remarkable characteristic of Darwin's *On the Origin of Species* is that it contains only one diagram and no other drawings, or statistical tables. The one diagram is what we now famously refer to as "the tree of life," a term that Darwin did not use. Darwin's diagram suggested that a few "simple" forms of life became the progenitors for all of life that we observe today. Today, we refer to the

---

[7] Darwin is referring to the philosopher Sir Francis Bacon (1561-1626), who many regard as the father of the modern scientific method of inquiry.

tree of life idea as *phylogeny*, a term credited to the German biologist and philosopher Ernst Haeckel (1834-1919). Haeckel embraced Darwin's theories and popularized Darwinian concepts among the German intellectual community of his day. In short, Darwin's tree of life, or phylogeny was a visual representation of descent with modification (1876/1998, p. 149).

The authors of *Theories of Everything*, published by the National Geographic Society rightly observed: "Philosopher Herbert Spencer coined the term "evolution" to refer to Darwin's theory, but the word did not appear in Charles Darwin's famous book, *The Origin of the Species*, until the 6th edition, 1872" (Langone, Stutz, & Gianopoulos, 2006, p. 258).

So how do we reconcile these observations? Darwin published his theory of descent with modification in 1859 in his book: *On the Origin of Species*. Today, no one talks about descent with modification, we talk about evolution and associate the term with Darwin. In addition, we discovered that Darwin published a total of six editions of his book *On the Origin of Species*; it was not until the final edition, that Darwin used the term *evolution*. Why did Darwin wait so long to use the term evolution, a term that is now indelibly etched into the minds of biologists everywhere as being associated with Darwin? To answer these questions, let us first find out more about Herbert Spencer.

The Philosopher, Herbert Spencer

Herbert Spencer (1820-1903) was a contemporary of Charles Darwin and was born in Derby, England. Spencer was a prolific writer who wrote on a variety of topics including, sociology, psychology, biology, and philosophy. Spencer was mainly self-educated and was an avid reader of scientific articles and books. As a result, he was well-versed on academic topics. In a paper called "The Development Hypothesis," Spencer lays out his theory of evolution in the following manner:

Those who cavalierly reject the Theory of Evolution[8] as not being adequately supported by facts, seem to forget that their own theory is supported by no facts at all. . . Well, which is the most rational theory about these ten millions of species? Is it most likely that there have been ten millions of special creations? Or is it most likely that, by continual modifications due to change of circumstances, ten millions of varieties have been produced, as varieties are being produced still? (Spencer, 1852, p. 1)

Many would recognize that there really is nothing remarkable in Spencer's observation and that it is very similar to French zoologist Jean-Baptiste Lamarck's (1744-1829) thesis that all living things today are descendants of simpler preceding forms, having been influenced by their environment. Lamarck published his views in his book: *Zoological Philosophy* (1809/1914). At the time, Lamarck's ideas were not received with much enthusiasm by the scientific community. In like manner, Spencer was not taken very seriously. Spencer coined the term *evolution* and applied it to Lamarck's theory, but Spencer's ideas also remained unconvincing. What Lamarck and Spencer both lacked was an agent of change; Darwin provided the causal agent in *natural selection*.

Remarkably, history often reflects ironic turns of fate. As it turned out, Spencer's term *evolution*, ultimately won the public relations battle. Darwin created the theory, *descent with modification*; however, the public preferred the term *evolution*. In the end, Spencer's term won the day and Darwin received the credit for its originality – a rather ironic twist of fate.

The late evolutionary biologist and Harvard professor Stephen Jay Gould observed that Herbert Spencer's term "evolution" replaced Darwin's term "descent with modification" in the following manner. According to Gould,

---

[8]   There is some evidence that the phrase was originally "Those who cavalierly reject the Theory of Lamarck." Spencer later republished this paper substituting "Evolution" for "Lamarck."

Darwin shunned evolution as a description for his descent with modification, both because its technical meaning contrasted his beliefs and because he was uncomfortable with the notion of inevitable progress inherent in its vernacular meaning. . . Evolution entered the English language as a synonym for "descent with modification" through the propaganda of Herbert Spencer, the indefatigable Victorian pundit of nearly everything. Evolution to Spencer, was the overarching law of all development. (Gould, 1977, p. 36)

Prior to Spencer, the term evolution had no meaning that was coupled to the field of biology. In Noah Webster's 1828 *American Dictionary of the English Language* we read the following definition for the word evolution: "(1) The act of unfolding or unrolling, (2) A series of things unrolled or unfolded; as the evolution of ages" (Webster, 1828/1983). The other definitions for evolution describe the word being used for geometry, algebra, and military tactics. Spencer used the term *evolution*, a term that had nothing to do with biology and applied it to *descent with modification*.

Spencer was a prolific writer and philosopher who tended to write in sweeping generalizations. Darwin was aware of Spencer's grandiose application of scientific principles. In his autobiography, Darwin commented on Spencer's methodology: "His [referring to Herbert Spencer] deductive manner of treating every subject is wholly opposed to my frame of mind" (Barlow, 2005, p. 131). It becomes clear that Darwin resisted the adoption of Spencer's substitution of Spencer's evolution for Darwin's descent with modification because Darwin was in opposition to Spencer's non-scientific methodology.

Spencer's broad-brush deductive approach has been criticized my numerous scholars. In the *Encyclopedia of Philosophy,* we read the following summary of Spencer's use of the term evolution:

Spencer's evolutionary theory covered too much. It did little to explain why evolution took one direction rather than another. Unlike scientific laws, his principle of evolution did not permit any genuine predictions. Any change whatsoever could be interpreted as a step in the evolutionary process, and therefore, no falsification of the principle could ever occur. . . It is fairly clear that the theory of evolution had the same logical status for Spencer as the dialectic had for Hegel: no evidence was to be allowed to repudiate the doctrine. (P. Edwards, 1967, p. 527)

Creating Theories and Defining Terms

When researchers, natural scientists, social scientists and philosophers propose new theories, they often create new technical terms. Benjamin Franklin created the term *battery*, to describe something that holds an electrical charge. The German philosopher Immanuel Kant used the terms *phenomenon* and *noumenon* to make distinctions in metaphysics regarding that which is known and that which is unknowable. Isaac Newton created a new mathematical method called *calculus* because he needed a way to describe and quantify his theories regarding gravity and motion.

In each of these examples we see that scientists and philosophers often, out of necessity, need to create new terms to describe the theory that they are postulating. Creating new terms and defining them is referred to as an operational definition. Isaac and Michael (1995) in their *Handbook in Research and Evaluation* defined *operational definition* as defining a "construct in terms of some form of objective procedure or measure that will yield a quantitative (numerical) designation of standing on a variable reflecting that construct" (p. 2). This is common in the behavioral sciences; define a term or a construct in a manner that can be observed and measured by other observers.

Although Darwin was not a social scientist, he followed the same principle. He created new terms, or constructs, and then attempted to define them in such a way that others could observe and validate his theories. This is the inductive scientific approach. Let's see how Darwin defined descent with modification.

Darwin Defines Descent with Modification

Very few biologists today use Darwin's original term *descent with modification*. Darwin took great pains to gather data and build his theory over a 20-year period. Here, Darwin (1876/1998) describes how descent with modification casts light on morphology and homology:

> On this same view of descent with modification, most of the great facts in Morphology become intelligible, - whether we look to the same pattern displayed by the different species of the same class in homologous organs, to whatever purpose applied; or to the serial and lateral homologies in each individual animal and plant. (p. 610)

Morphology refers to the structure and form of living organisms. The Swedish naturalist and botanist Carolus Linnaeus (1707-1778) used the principles of morphology to create his *Linnean hierarchy* which classifies organisms by "the degree of their similarity and relationship" (Mayr, 2001, p. 23). The term *homology* refers to a similarity in structure between different species and is used as evidence for descent with modification (Mayr, 2001, p. 25). An example of homology would be a similarity in bone structure between a human hand and a cat's paw.

Herbert Spencer Advances the Term Evolution

Where did the term evolution originate? Charles Darwin and Alfred Wallace (1858) published the paper "On the tendency of species to form varieties; and on the perpetuation of varieties and species by natural means of selection." In that paper, the term *natural selection* was used three times and the term *evolution* was never used. Darwin did not use the term *evolution* until the 6th and final edition of *The Origin of Species* (Darwin, 1876)!

Herbert Spencer is generally credited for coining the term *evolution* and using it in a biological sense. Prior to Spencer, *evolution*

– meant "the act of unfolding or unrolling" (Webster, 1828/1983). Spencer is credited with giving the term *evolution* a biological meaning prior to Charles Darwin. Spencer wrote a paper called the "Development Hypothesis" (1852) in which he used the term *evolution* and proposed that the theory of special creation was insufficient. In that paper, Spencer asked the question: "is it most likely that, by continual modifications due to change of circumstances, ten millions of varieties have been produced, as varieties are being produced still?" In addition, Herbert Spencer discussed "the evolution of life" (p. 6) in his book *Principles of Psychology* (1855) and used the term evolution numerous times. Spencer was using evolution in a biological sense, three to five years before Charles Darwin.

In contrast, Charles Darwin and Alfred Russel Wallace (1858), published a theory of natural selection with the Linnean Society. Darwin felt that Wallace's methods of observation and scientific induction were sound. In contrast, Darwin cared little for Spencer's deductive system of logic; Darwin preferred inductive reasoning and the scientific method pioneered by Francis Bacon. Nevertheless, Spencer continued his quest to replace *descent with modification* with the term *evolution*. Seven years after Darwin published his *On the Origin of Species* (1859), Spencer continued to advance the term *evolution* in his book *The Principles of Biology* (1866). Spencer writes,

> The aim of this work is to set forth the general truths of Biology, as illustrative of, and as Interpreted by, the laws of Evolution: the special truths being introduced only so far as is needful for elucidation of the general truths. (Spencer, 1866, p. Preface to Eng. Ed.)

In the end, Spencer's term, *evolution* became more popular than Darwin's theory of *descent with modification*. It is perhaps one of the greatest paradoxes in the annals of modern scientific discovery. Where Darwin was specific, Spencer was characteristically vague.

Where Darwin used *inductive reasoning*[9], Spencer used *deductive reasoning*[10]. Where Darwin took painstaking measures to produce evidence for his theories, Spencer was content to produce very little direct evidence, relying instead on generalizations and analogies.

Here is how Spencer defined *evolution* in his book *First Principles*: "It is true that Evolution, under its primary aspect, is a change from a less coherent form to a more coherent form, consequent on the dissipation of motion and integration of matter" (Spencer, 1862/1898, p. 370). Spencer also preferred the term "The Law of Evolution." Spencer preferred the grandiose to the more subtle and circumscribed scientific methodology. At the conclusion of the chapter titled "The Law of Evolution," Spencer restates his definition: "As we now understand it, Evolution is definable as a change from an incoherent homogeneity to a coherent heterogeneity, accompanying the dissipation of motion and integration of matter" (Spencer, 1862/1898, p. 371).

Spencer set out to argue and defend principles that could neither be defended nor supported. In short, Spencer's methodology was to argue from *a priori*[11] principles to arrive at a sweeping conclusion. Spencer could do this because he was not a scientist; he was a philosopher. Spencer described science in the following manner: "What is Science? To see the absurdity of the prejudice against it, we need only remark that Science is simply a higher development of common knowledge; and that if Science is repudiated, all knowledge must be repudiated along with it." (Spencer, 1862/1898, p. 18).

---

[9]   *The American Heritage Dictionary* defines **induction** as: "The act or process of deriving general principles from particular facts or instances" (Morris, 1982, p. 657). The process of induction became formalized as the *scientific method* by Sir Francis Bacon (1561-1626) (Langone et al., 2006, p. 251).

[10]   *The American Heritage Dictionary* defines **deduction** as: In many ways is the antithesis of inductive reasoning. "The process of reasoning in which a conclusion follows necessarily from the stated premises, inference by reasoning from the general to the specific" (Morris, 1982, p. 373)

[11]   *a priori* is Latin for, "from before." *The American Heritage Dictionary* defines **a priori** as, "made before or without examination; not supported by factual study" (Morris, 1982, p. 122).

Spencer's definition of science is nothing like the scientific method described by Francis Bacon (1561-1626). Bacon was the first to propose a clear scientific method based on repeated experimentation with the eventual goal of forming testable theories. Scientific laws were thus the result of an inductive method of reasoning, which could be verified or falsified by others (Durant, 2005; Magee, 2001). Bacon's scientific method was nothing like Spencer's.

In contrast, Spencer's idea of science was more of a theory of knowledge, or a metaphysical approach to knowledge. Spencer's research completely lacked any experimental methodology or repeatable verification; he did not use Bacon's scientific method.

Why is it important to understand the difference between the terms *descent with modification* and *evolution*? Aren't these two terms interchangeable?

Do Descent with Modification and Evolution mean the Same Thing?

If the terms *descent with modification* and *evolution* are clearly synonymous, then asking if they have identical meanings is a useless exercise. If, however, the terms are not identical, then the very meaning of Darwin's theory is altered by Spencer's substitution. The following exercise demonstrates how a person's worldview can be affected by the words that we speak and use regularly.

Human communication theorists Sapir and Whorf postulated that human beings are bound by language. This is known as the Sapir-Whorf hypothesis. In other words, our language reflects our culture and our culture defines who we are. Communication scholar Littlejohn summed up the Sapir-Whorf hypothesis this way: "This hypothesis suggests that our thought processes and the way we see the world are shaped by the grammatical structure of the language" (Littlejohn, 2002, p. 177).

Let us now test the terms *evolution* (A) and *descent with modification* (B) using the Sapir-Whorf hypothesis. If the meanings of the two terms are identical, then if A = B, then the substitution of A for B will yield no change in meaning. However, If A is substituted for

B and the meaning changes, then we must reject the hypothesis that A=B and conclude that the terms A and B are not identical.

In the following passage, Darwin (1876/1998) notes that his theory will be challenged: "That many and serious objections may be advanced against the theory of descent with modification through variation and natural selection, I do not deny" (p. 612).

If we substitute *evolution* for *descent with modification*, the passage still makes sense: "That many and serious objections may be advanced against the theory of ~~descent with modification~~ [evolution] through variation and natural selection, I do not deny."

However, if we turn to a modern passage published by the National Academy of Sciences (2008) using the term *evolution*, we find that the terms are no longer interchangeable:

> The evidence for evolution comes not just from the biological sciences but also from both historical and modern research in anthropology, astrophysics, chemistry, geology, physics, mathematics, and other scientific disciplines, including the behavioral and social sciences. (p. 17)

Again, let's make a substitution, as Sapir-Whorf suggest. If the terms *evolution* and *descent with modification* are synonymous, then the following passage should make sense if *evolution* is replaced by *descent with modification*.

> The evidence for ~~evolution~~ [descent with modification] comes not just from the biological sciences but also from both historical and modern research in anthropology, astrophysics, chemistry, geology, physics, mathematics, and other scientific disciplines, including the behavioral and social sciences. (National Academy of Sciences and Institute of Medicine., 2008, p. 17)

With this change, the quotation is now saying that descent with modification is supported with evidence from biology, anthropology, astrophysics, chemistry, geology, physics, mathematics, psychology and the social sciences! Darwin was very specific that descent with modification (DWM) was a theory of development of living things. DWM proposed that living things changed from generation to generation over time. The fields of astrophysics, psychology and the social sciences do not yield data that support DWM. Astrophysics does not deal with living things. Psychology is the study of human behavior; it does not address other living things. The social sciences, address human society, not animals.

Let's think about term substitution critically. Do we truly believe that stars compete with each other the same way that two dogs fight over a bone? Does it sound reasonable that hydrogen competes with oxygen for the position at the top of the periodic table of elements? Do rocks compete with each other (for who knows what)? Do mathematical concepts compete with mathematical concepts (this makes no sense)? How is it possible for inanimate substances that are not alive such as minerals, rocks, and stars, to compete with each other? How is it possible for incorporeal[12] concepts such as mathematics to compete with mathematics? If the term *descent with modification* is substituted for the term *evolution* in the above quotation, the meaning of the passage becomes so obscured that it falls somewhere between the absurd and the ridiculous.

If Sapir and Whorf are correct, and we are bound by the words that we speak, and understand; then, Spencer's definition of evolution is a fundamental shift in thinking compared to the Darwinian term *descent with modification*. While this point may seem to be miniscule to some, it is quite revolutionary. By substituting the term evolution for *descent with modification*, Spencer changed the meaning of Darwin's theory.

Darwin strove to create a naturalistic explanation for life on earth. In contrast, Spencer advanced a theory that redefined modern man in relation to the entire universe. Darwin sought to establish a scientific testable theory; Spencer sought to establish a new metaphysical reality *a priori*. In other words, Spencer did not have to provide any evidence; he simply needed to assume that his theory

---

12   *The American Heritage Dictionary* defines *incorporeal* as, "lacking material form or substance." (Morris, 1982, p. 652). Latin for without (not) + body.

was true. Therefore, Spencer (1862/1898, p. Chapter 14) used the term "The Law of Evolution."

Darwin was clearly suspicious of Spencer's sweeping generalizations and method of deductive reasoning. Here, Darwin clarifies his opposition to Spencer's methodology:

> Nevertheless I am not conscious of having profited in my own work by Spencer's writings. His deductive manner of treating every subject is wholly opposed to my frame of mind. His conclusions never convince me: and over and over again I have said to myself, after reading one of his discussions, - "Here would be a fine subject for half-a-dozen year's work." His fundamental generalizations (which have been compared in importance by some persons with Newton's Laws!) – which I daresay may be very valuable under a philosophical point of view, are of such a nature that they do not seem to me to be of any strictly scientific use. . . They do not aid one in predicting what will happen in any particular case. Anyhow they have not been of any use to me. (Barlow, 2005, p. 90)

Can the Inductive Method be applied to Descent with Modification?

This is the critical question that we have been leading up to. We have already discussed that fact that Darwin was a man of science and that he resisted Spencer's reframing of the theory of descent with modification into the theory of evolution. We have shown that the term *evolution* cannot be substituted for *descent with modification*, since the first term uses deductive reasoning, while the second uses inductive logic.

Let us now for the sake of argument fall back on the original premise that was presented by Darwin and use an inductive approach to gather evidence for descent with modification. Let us use "Baconian principles" (Barlow, 2005, p. 98) as Darwin said he did, in order to gather evidence to support the hypothesis of descent with modification.

Herein lies the problem, for there is a distinction between microevolution and macroevolution. Professor of Geology, Donald Prothero (2007a) explains,

> This defines all evolution as *microevolution,* the gradual and tiny changes that cause different wing veins in a fruit fly or a slightly longer tail in a rat. From this, Neo-Darwinism extrapolates all larger evolutionary changes (macroevolution) as just microevolution writ large. (p. 94)

No one disputes the observation of microevolution, a process that is "at or below the species level" (Mayr, 2001, p. 287). There are hundreds of varieties of cats, dogs and other household pets. This is without dispute. But on the topic of macroevolution, the evidence is less clear. As Harvard Professor of Zoology Ernst Mayr (2001) defines *macroevolution* as taking place "above the species level; the evolution of higher taxa and the production of evolutionary novelties, such as new structures" (287).

Once again, the inductive method is what we refer to as the scientific method (or Baconian method). Using induction, hypotheses are formulated, data are observed, and through careful observation and experimentation a particular hypothesis is either supported or rejected. The wise scientist prefers the term *supported* to *proven,* since one does not know if future experimentation with new data will render the hypothesis invalid.

Let's now apply the inductive method to human beings. We can trace human existence back in time a few thousand years. We have written records of births and deaths. We also have oral histories of genealogies in poems, songs and literature. The Jewish culture can trace their lineage back to the first man, Adam. Other cultures, such as those in ancient Egypt, India, China, South America, can also trace back their human ancestors thousands of years. The problem is that at a certain point we reach a dead end; the records only go back so far into the past.

Neo-Darwinists today tell us that human beings are descendants of some early form of man that came from Africa. The problem with this theory is that it is supported by inference and not direct observation. We have no primary sources such as witnesses, photo-graphs, or birth records to verify that modern man is the descendant of a proposed progenitor of Homo sapiens.

In this sense, the inductive method fails because the chain of evidence is broken. We have no direct evidence of modern man being related to *Australopithecus* or other extinct hominids that lived millions of years ago. No one has observed the assumed unbroken chain of births and deaths between Australopithecus and modern Homo sapiens. The conclusion is based solely upon an inference. Even more disturbing is the fact that the inference is now considered *a priori* evidence by most biologists! Ironically, modern biology has committed the same fallacy of deductive reasoning that Darwin so adamantly criticized as being advanced by Herbert Spencer!

The fact is that modern scientists *must* conclude that Homo sapiens are the descendants of early hominids such as Australopithecus because modern biology is committed to the Darwinian world-view or epistemology. In short, modern Darwinists (also called neo-Darwinists) are committed more to an ideology, than an inductive scientific approach to knowledge.

The irony is that, among Neo-Darwinists there is no logical inconsistency since the community of scholars has reached a unanimous conclusion. Any other explanation other than a naturalistic, materialistic, reductionistic, Darwinian schema would be anathema to western academia. If one is committed to a philosophy of materialistic reductionism, then there can be no other explanation. Geologist Donald Prothero (2007a) explains that Neo-Darwinists subscribe to the following belief system:

These central tenants – reductionism, panselectionism, extrapolationism, and gradualism – were central to the Neo-Darwinian orthodoxy of the 1940s and 1950s and are still followed by the majority of evolutionary biologists today" (p. 94)

Chapter Summary

This chapter discussed the myth that Charles Darwin created a theory called evolution by focusing on the terms *descent with modification* and *evolution*. Charles Darwin published his theory of descent with modification in 1858 with Alfred Russel Wallace. Then, in 1859 Darwin published his much more exhaustive work as *On the Origin of Species by Means of Natural Selection: Or, the Preservation of Favored Races in the Struggle for Life*.

The result of Darwin's publication upon the scientific community was revolutionary, even though it was not without its critics. Darwin went on to publish six editions of his *On the Origin of Species* and we learned that remarkably the term *evolution* was not used until the very last edition of the same work. It is quite clear that Darwin did not use the term evolution when he first published his theory in 1858 and 1859 because it did not appear in print in either of these publications.

It was Herbert Spencer who advanced the term *evolution* which eventually replaced Darwin's *theory of descent with modification*. Biologist Stephen Jay Gould paints Spencer as the villain in this scientific drama. Curiously, Gould (1977) concluded that "since most evolutionists saw organic change as a process directed toward increasing complexity (that is, to us) their appropriation of Spencer's general term did no violence to his definition" (p. 37).

I must disagree with Gould's conclusion that Spencer's substitution of terms "did no violence" to Darwin's definition. Indeed, I have demonstrated using the Sapir-Whorf hypothesis and logical substitution, that the terms *descent with modification* and *evolution* are not interchangeable.

The result of Spencer's substitution is that a theory that began with inductive scientific reasoning morphed into a theory-of-everything, using grandiose deductive philosophical claims. Clearly, this is not what Darwin envisioned. At the end of day, both Darwin and Spencer won out. Darwin used the term *evolution* in his 6th edition of *On the Origin of Species* and history credits Darwin for the theory and the term. Spencer took a back seat in terms of historical significance, but his deductive approach prevailed – in spite of Darwin's disapproval.

In the end, there is a subtle irony in this exercise of substitution of terms. Mr. Herbert Spencer (1898) was not able to correct the "prevailing misapprehension" (p. vi) that Darwin coined the term *evolution*. On the other hand, the term *evolution* has now become exactly what Spencer intended and Darwin did not: Evolution has become a sweeping world view, a philosophy that embraces all aspects of scientific enquiry. Evolution, as it is applied today, is not simply a biological theory. Evolution is an epistemological lens, a way of knowing the world.

Finally, we applied the scientific method (or inductive approach) to observations related to the development of Homo sapiens on earth. We discovered that at some point direct observations and primary evidence will cease. We can only go so far back in time with direct records of births and deaths. We may be able to go back a few millennia, at best. However, this is a trifle when compared to an unbroken chain of life and death from the pre-Cambrian period leading to the development of Homo sapiens. Therefore, we have concluded that this sort of logic is not inductive. It is deductive at best and specious at worst.

At the beginning of this chapter I asked the question, "Why does it matter who came up with the term *evolution*?" It does matter, because as Sapir-Whorf postulated – we are bound by our language and our ideas; we cannot escape our words, they define us. The scientific theory that Darwin proposed: Descent with Modification (DWM) is out, and so is inductive reasoning when it comes to Darwinian biology. What replaced DWM was a deductive theory that was advanced by Spencer, the theory we now refer to as *evolution*.

Some may argue that this is only a trivial substitution of terms, I have demonstrated in this chapter that scientific definitions are not trivial and that by replacing *descent with modification* (DWM) with the term *evolution*, all biological research from that point forward was changed. Evolution has become a ubiquitous term being applied to natural science, social science, astrophysics, cosmology and more. By rejecting Darwin's theory of DWM and substituting Spencer's term of *evolution*, scientists are today forced to work from the starting point of an elusive philosophical theory of everything! Perhaps, the late evolutionary biologist Stephen Jay Gould put it best in his criticism of Spencer's deductive approach when Gould (1977) referred to Spencer as, "that indefatigable Victorian pundit of nearly everything" (p. 36).

II. Myth 2: Natural Selection is the Primary Cause of Macro Evolution

Natural selection is the central concept of Darwinian theory – the fittest survive and spread their favored traits through populations.
Paleontologist Stephen Jay Gould (1977, p.40)

Macroevolution - Evolution above the species level; the evolution of higher taxa and the production of evolutionary novelties, such as new structures.
Evolutionary biologist Ernst Mayr (2001, p. 287)

Darwin had two grand ideas; descent with modification (DWM) and natural selection. DWM was an improvement from what the great French botanist Jean-Baptiste Lamarck (1744-1829) proposed. Lamarck's theory was that simpler biological forms were the progenitors of more complex forms of life and that *time* and *environment* produced the changes that we see in the variety of life forms that exist today. Lamarck's theories were not well received. In contrast, Darwin seemed to provide a more convincing argument to the scientific community.

As we discussed in the previous chapter, Darwin improved upon Lamarck's hypothesis by suggesting a process called descent with modification (DWM) – the idea that traits are passed on from generation to generation and that all living things are the result of their prior ancestors. Today, DWM has been reframed by the neo-Darwinism movement of the 1940s and 50's with seemingly bountiful scientific evidence from the study of genetics. In addition to DWM, Darwin knew that he needed to identify an essential driving force behind change. Darwin did not want to make the same mistake that Lamarck had made; he did not want to propose a theory of biological origins that had no cause. Darwin proposed cause for biological change in his second grand idea.

The second grand idea was *natural selection*. Darwin proposed that something called *natural selection* (and not time and environment as Lamarck proposed) was the driving force behind DWM. Natural selection suggested that living things compete with other living things for survival. This competition may be either in the form of males competing for mating rights or by physical characteristics that make one form of life more suitable to survival than another. Darwin suggested that advantageous physical characteristics were the product of undirected mutations over time. History records that Darwin's idea was well received during his lifetime.

In this chapter, I will be discussing natural selection in more detail. I will challenge the notion that natural selection is the primary cause of macro evolution. In the first part of this chapter we will be looking at how Darwin formulated his theory of natural selection. We will also see how Herbert Spencer was once again influential, by modifying Darwin's theory of natural selection.[13]

In the second part of the chapter we discuss challenges to natural selection. We will be examining the new field of evolutionary development (evo-devo) and catastrophism. Catastrophism is a force that acts without discrimination upon all living things. Let us begin with how Darwin formulated his theory of natural selection.

Malthus and the Path to Natural Selection

Darwin was both meticulous and patient in his gathering of data. He was determined to not commit the same errors that Lamarck

---

[13]   In chapter one, we discussed how it was Herbert Spencer that proposed a theory called *evolution*. Darwin's original theory was called *descent with modification*.

did before him. Darwin reasoned that Lamarck's theory that environmental change was a driving force behind changes in species over time was unconvincing. Darwin knew that he needed a more profound idea on which to hinge his theory of descent with modification. Darwin was a prolific reader of scientific literature. One day, he read a scholarly paper by Thomas Malthus, on the study of populations.

Who was Malthus? Thomas Robert Malthus (1766–1834) was a British economist and professor of political economy. The paper that Darwin read was titled: *An Essay on the Principle of Population* (Malthus, 1798). In that essay, Malthus argued that human populations grew and either flourished or declined in relation to the available food supply. If the food supply increased, then populations increased. If the food supply was curtailed, then populations would diminish as the result of famine or war. Malthus further reasoned that populations both of humans and animals will grow exponentially if left unrestrained. In time, Malthus reasoned, the earth would not be able to sustain such unrestrained growth because of limited food supplies. This is how Darwin described his exposure to the thoughts of Malthus:

> In October 1838, that is, fifteen months after I had begun my systematic enquiry, I happened to read for amusement Malthus on *Population*, and being well prepared to appreciate the struggle for existence which everywhere goes on from long-continued observations of the habits of animals and plants, it at once struck me that under these circumstances favourable [*sic*] variations would tend to be preserved, and unfavourable [*sic*] ones to be destroyed. The result of this would be the formation of new species. Here, then, I had at last got a theory by which to work . . . (Barlow, 2005, pp. 98-99)

Darwin went on to explain in his autobiography that he took time to form his theory before he published his ideas. He began writing his theory of natural selection in 1842 and did not fully develop it until 1844 (Barlow, 2005). This was the argument that Darwin was searching for;

it was a natural process that Darwin used to explain changes in living things over time. Darwin would call this process *natural selection;* it would be the driving force behind descent with modification.

Lamarck and others had failed to formulate a credible theory to explain how new species developed over time. Darwin, on the other hand, created a new theory that contained a plausible explanation for the development of new species over time. Thanks to Malthus, Darwin found his causal force in nature – natural selection. Let us now discuss how Darwin defined natural selection.

Darwin Defines Natural Selection

Darwin argued that natural selection is the cause, while descent with modification (DWM) is the resulting effect. The establishment of a cause and effect relationship between natural selection and DWM is critical to Darwin's theory. Darwin (1876/1998) makes the causal link between his two theories in the following statement: "That many and serious objections may be advanced against the theory of descent with modification through variation and natural selection, I do not deny" (p. 612).

The full title of Darwin's book is: *The Origin of Species: By Means of Natural Selection Or the Preservation of Favored Races in the Struggle for Life* (Darwin, 1859). As was common with many scientific published works, the authors of such works did not strive for parsimony when crafting titles. Darwin was making it clear in the title that a process called natural selection was the driving force in the struggle for life. Here are a few definitions that Darwin (1876/1998) gave for *natural selection*. This definition outlines the struggle for existence:

> The theory of natural selection is grounded on the belief that each new variety and ultimately each new species, is produced and maintained by having some advantage over those which it comes into competition; and the consequent extinction of the less-favoured [*sic*] forms almost inevitably follows. (p. 452)

Here is another definition of natural selection. In this second definition, Darwin mentions Herbert Spencer. Spencer seemed to have a flair for rhetorical expression and a desire to want to assist Darwin in the description of his theories. In the following passage, Darwin credits Spencer with the invention of the phrase "survival of the fittest." This passage appeared in the sixth and final edition of *On the Origin of Species*:

> Again, it may be asked, how is it that varieties, which I have called incipient species, become ultimately converted into good and distinct species which in most cases obviously differ from each other far more than do the varieties of the same species? . . . I have called this principle, by which each slight variation, if useful, is preserved, by the term Natural Selection, in order to mark its relation to man's power of selection. But the expression often used by Mr. Herbert Spencer of the Survival of the Fittest is more accurate, and is sometimes equally convenient. (Darwin, 1876/1998, p. 88)

Spencer Redefines Natural Selection

Darwin was a scientist who sought out causal relationships through observation of natural phenomena. In his autobiography, Darwin describes his process of reasoning in the following manner: "I worked on Baconian principles, and without any theory collected facts on a wholesale scale" (Barlow, 2005, p. 98).

Here, Darwin is referring to Francis Bacon (1561-1626), a philosopher who is credited with creating a methodology for the modern scientific method. Bacon proposed that data should first be gathered, theories could be formed to explain the data, predictions could be made based on theories and other researchers should be able to test the theories by independently gathering new data. Modern science is based on the notion that proper research occurs when others can independently repeat the process and observe similar results.

Francis Bacon also had a vision for the formation of scientific societies. Eventually, the Royal Society was formed in 1662, after

Bacon's death. It was the Royal Society which later helped to propel many of Darwin's ideas forward in the scientific community.

We discussed Spencer's deductive and *a priori* approach to scientific principles in Chapter One. *A priori* is Latin for, "of before." In philosophy, *a priori* statements do not need to be proven; rather, they are assumed to be true. Interestingly, Spencer was not cited in the first edition of *On the Origin of Species*. However, by the sixth edition, Darwin mentions Spencer six times!

Perhaps Darwin was a bit irritated by Spencer's constant tinkering with Darwin's theories and rhetorical choices. In an extremely clever and gracious gesture, Darwin resorts to flattery to tempt Spencer to return to the field of psychology and leave biology to others. In this, I must give Darwin credit, Spencer had hounded Darwin for years and yet Darwin chose to complement Spencer, hoping that Spencer would take the compliment and resume his research in psychology. Here are Darwin's words in relation to Herbert Spencer:

> In the future I see open fields for far more important researches. Psychology will be securely based on the foundation already well laid by Mr. Herbert Spencer, that of the necessary acquirement of each mental power and capacity by gradation. Much light will be thrown on the origin of man and his history. (Darwin, 1876/1998, p. 647)

To summarize, Darwin was inspired by the writings of Malthus to create a theory of natural selection – which became the driving force for Darwin's theory of descent with modification. Spencer modified natural selection by introducing the concept of "survival of the fittest," a phrase that Darwin credited to Spencer in his sixth edition of *On the Origin of Species*.

Natural selection has been discussed in great detail for over a century and as evolutionary geologist Donald Prothero recounts, prior to the 1930s natural selection was in serious doubt as being the driving factor behind evolution. It was not until the 1930s that *population genetics* theory emerged as a way of reconciling Mendel's genetic discoveries with Darwin's theory of natural selection. Prothero (2007a) summarizes the situation as follows:

. . . there appeared to be no way to show that Darwinian natural selection was compatible with genetics, paleontology, and systematics[14]. The breakthrough occurred in the 1930s, when three scientists introduced a set of mathematical models known as *population genetics*. . .These mathematical model simulations allowed evolutionists to describe changing gene frequencies through many generations and simulate the effects of mutation and selection. Population genetics clearly showed that even slight selection pressure can quickly change gene frequencies and made evolution by Darwinian natural selection plausible again. . . After almost 50 years, most current evolution textbooks still reflect this dominance of Neo-Darwinism. (p. 93)

Two important points need to be highlighted. First, prior to the 1930s, natural selection as the driving force for evolution was not universally accepted in the scientific community. Ironically, one of the problems with the theory of natural selection was the discovery of the new science of genetics, which is attributed to the research of an Austrian Monk, Gregor Johann Mendel (1822–1884). As a monk, Mendel was a believer in God; the irony of history is that Mendel's research is often used by professed atheists such as Richard Dawkins (2006), author of *The God Delusion*, to advance Darwinian dogma.

As the geologist Donald Prothero pointed out, prior to the 1930s there was conflict between *genetics* (the study of the heredity and variation of organisms), *paleontology* (the study of past geological periods through fossil remains), and *systematics* (the naming and relationships of organisms through time). This is not necessarily a bad thing, for it is controversy and disagreement in science that leads to new research and often new discoveries.

Secondly, in the 1930s, three mathematicians created mathematical models which became known as *population genetics* (Prothero, 2007a, p. 93). These mathematicians were R.A. Fisher, J.B.S. Haldane and Sewall Wright (Okasha, 2012). Mathematical

---

[14]   Systematists is the field of biology that studies and names relationships of organisms.

models derived by Fisher, Haldane and Sewall sought reconciliation between the opposing Mendelian geneticists and Darwinists who could not agree that Gregor Mendel's genetic discoveries were compatible with Darwin's theory of natural selection. In time, population genetics was eventually accepted, but it took a few decades. The new unity between biologists became known as *neo-Darwinism.*

Here are the foundational truths of the Neo-Darwinist dogma as described by evolutionary geologist Donald Prothero (2007a):

> These central tenets – reductionism, panselectionism, extrapolism, and gradualism – were central to the Neo-Darwinian orthodoxy of the 1940s and 1950s and are still followed by the majority of evolutionary biologists today. (p. 94)

Neo-Darwinism is clearly reductionist, it asserts *a priori* that all life on earth is the result of a common ancestor. As a naturalistic framework, neo-Darwinism excludes the metaphysical and the spiritual dimensions entirely. In addition, neo-Darwinism assumes that all animal and human behavior can be explained from a naturalistic point of view. This means that metaphysical theories such as Cartesian dualism[15] or any other attempt to embrace a theory of human beings being a combination of physical and soul (or physical and spiritual) are also rejected *a priori* by Neo-Darwinists.

Even though neo-Darwinism seemed to resolve the conflicts that swirled around natural selection in the 1930s, modern evolutionary biology is not without controversy. There is a small group of evolutionary biologists that have developed a new theory that is intended to unseat natural selection as the driving force behind descent with modification.

---

[15]   This refers to the philosophy of French mathematician Rene Descartes (1596-1650). Descartes proposed that humans were dualistic or two-part beings, being composed of body and soul.

Evolutionary Development Theory

This relatively new theory is referred to as *evolutionary development* or Evo/Devo for short. Evolutionary development has developed because new tools used in genetic research and the study of embryonic development were developed. Scientists that study evolutionary development strive to understand how multi-cellular life develops from the single cell and then diversifies into the millions of different cells that make up multi-celled living things. Darwin did not ask these sorts of questions since the field of microbiology did not exist during his time.

Evolutionary biologist Ralf Sommer (2009) defined evolutionary development (evo-devo) in the following manner: "Evolutionary developmental biology (evo–devo) investigates the evolution of developmental processes, aiming for a mechanistic understanding of phenotypic[16] change" (p. 416).

Let's summarize what has been discussed so far. Darwin created a theory called descent with modification (DWM). DWM advanced the idea that all present-day living things are descendants of past living things; over time there have been modifications and these modified traits have been passed down from generation to generation. The French botanist, Jean-Baptiste Lamarck (1744-1829) proposed a similar idea before Darwin published his *On the Origin of Species* in 1859. Lamarck's theories fell by the wayside, but Darwin's had momentum, since Darwin proposed that natural selection was the driving force behind descent with modification.

Today, *natural selection* is universally accepted and taught in high school text books as being the driving force behind descent with modification, today more commonly referred to as evolution. However, this was not the case. We discovered that natural selection was not accepted by most biologists as being the driving force of evolution until the 1930s when the new doctrine of neo-Darwinism emerged. We conclude, therefore, that natural selection was on shaky ground for the first sixty years after its initial proposal in 1859.

---

[16]   The observable physical characteristics of an organism.

Today, natural selection is once again being challenged. It is being challenged by *evolutionary development* theory or evo-devo – the study of the development of multi-cellular organisms from the embryonic stage through maturity. Evo-Devo is now gaining momentum even though it has not unseated natural selection as the driving force of evolution. Evo-devo is still a new field of research, and as Zoologist Wallace Arthur (2011) points out in his article, "Searching for evo-devo's Holy Grail: the nature of developmental variation" scientists are asking the question "is developmental variation structured?" This question has not yet been answered decisively; however, the research question drives scientists to conduct further research.

Finally, evo-devo is asking some questions that Darwin simply brushed by. For example: "How did development originate?" (Müller, 2007). Curiously, the answers to the origin of the genetic code may be metaphysical. The reason is self-evident, since a genetic code is information; a code is without substance and is incorporeal (without body). The committed reductionist is at a dead end when faced with the question: Where does the information come from?

Will evo-devo eventually unseat natural selection as the driving force behind descent with modification (a.k.a. evolution)? Only time will tell. It is the nature of science to continually evaluate the data and to formulate new theories to try and explain new scientific data. Often, new data arrive because scientists create new tools to observe and gather data. The invention of the telescope led to the Copernican revolution. The new science of genetics and the electron microscope have led to a multitude of discoveries in microbiology. This is the scientific process that was set forth by the English philosopher Francis Bacon (1561-1626).

Perhaps there are a variety of forces that drive biological change. We have already discussed the possibility that evo-devo is threatening natural selection as the force behind descent with modification. Is there a second force that can also unseat natural selection? The answer to that question is, yes. This second natural force is one that Darwin was extremely familiar with. With the assistance of the great biologist of Darwin's time, Charles Lyell, Darwin successfully argued to marginalize catastrophic terrestrial activity. This is a powerful lesson in public rhetoric. During his time, Lyell was above question, his views on geology were taken as definitive. It was not until over 100 years later that Lyell was successfully challenged by a physicist named Luis Alvarez.

Catastrophism versus Uniformitarianism

Catastrophes affect all living things on earth. Before Darwin proposed that changes occur in a fairly stable environment over long periods of time, scientists and scholars universally accepted the notion that catastrophes drove environmental change. This was borne out of direct observation passed down through both oral and written documentation. The eruption of the volcano Thera on the island of Santorini between 1645 and 1500 B.C, had the force of hundreds of atomic bombs. This catastrophe is credited for destroying the Minoan civilization and leading to the rise of the Greek city states (Friedrich, 2000).

Ancient cultures around the world have a long tradition of a catastrophic flood stories that caused cities such as the fabled Atlantis to vanish suddenly beneath the seas. In a 2012 article in *National Geographic News*, two recently discovered underwater civilizations were reported (Handwerk, 2012).

First, unexplained geological structures were discovered off the coast of Cuba in waters over 2000 feet deep by a Canadian exploration company - Advanced Digital Communications. Follow-up dives are scheduled to confirm if these are indeed man-made structures. Cuban geologist Manuel Iturralde wants to investigate further, since he cannot explain the structures geologically.

Second, in Tamil Nadu, South India, off the coast of Mahabalipuram, an ancient temple has been located that is completely submerged, under the sea. Monty Halls, the expedition leader reported what the local fisherman had known for centuries:

The initial feeling was one of disbelief," Halls recalled. "The sheer scale of the site was so impressive, and the fact that it was so close to shore. This gradually gave way to absolute elation. (Handwerk, 2012)

More recently, the volcanic explosion of the island of Krakatoa in August 1883 was a worldwide cataclysmic event. The explosion of the volcano reduced the land mass of the island from 18 square miles to 6 square miles. The volcano caused a tremendous tsunami that resulted in the drowning deaths of 34,000 people living on the shorelines of Java and Sumatra ("Krakatoa," 2001). The force of the explosion is estimated to be the equivalent of 200 megatons of TNT (Clary & Wandersee, 2011). Ash from the explosion circled the world and observations were made in Europe; people noted the appearance of beautiful colors in the sky in the morning and the evening (Schroder, 1999).

The Last Glacial Maximum (LGM) peaked about 21,500 years ago with ice sheets that advanced across North America, across the present day Great Lakes and reached into the Great Central Plains. It was thought that sheets of ice advanced and retreated slowly. In a recent television broadcast on CNN, ice was recorded on television advancing so rapidly that it could be seen moving in real time; the event was recorded by a television camera (Lendon, 2013). The rapid advancement of the ice was propelled by a very strong wind blowing across a large frozen lake in Minnesota. The moving ice destroyed numerous homes on Mille Lacs Lake, Minnesota; the ice flow was as high as 30 feet in some places. The ice moved 60 to 80 feet onshore across a 2.5-mile shoreline area.

Catastrophism is the antithesis of *uniformitarianism* – a slow geological change of the Earth's crust and climate. Rapidly advancing ice, a volcanic eruption, an earthquake, a tsunami or a collision from a comet or meteor are certainly not slow gradual events! *Catastrophism* is defined in the *Columbia Electronic Dictionary* as:

> . . . the doctrine that at intervals in the earth's history all living things have been destroyed by cataclysms (e.g., floods or earthquakes) and replaced by an entirely different population. During these cataclysms the features of the

earth's surface, such as mountains and valleys, were formed. ("Catastrophism," 2013)

This is what the geologist Clarence King (1877) refers to as the traditional definition of catastrophism. A view that suggests that the earth has been subject to numerous worldwide cataclysms that were of such strength and magnitude that both the geological features of the earth and the subsequent changes to the atmosphere were so radical and instantaneous that all life on earth was suddenly extinguished. For life to continue on earth it was thus necessary for new life forms to spring forth.

The theory of catastrophism was upheld (in various forms) for millennia and was later considered to be in harmony with the teachings of the church in Europe, which held to a literal interpretation of the worldwide flood of Noah's generation. But even before the Christian era, catastrophism was universally accepted by the scholarly community. The Greek philosopher Plato (360 B.C.) tells the following story of the demise of Atlantis from *Timaeus*.

But afterwards there occurred violent earthquakes and floods; and in a single day and night of misfortune all your warlike men in a body sank into the earth, and the island of Atlantis in like manner disappeared in the depths of the sea. (Plato, 360 B.C.E.)

Catastrophism was challenged by the British geologist James Hutton (1726-1797) who proposed a uniformitarian theory of geology, suggesting that natural processes such as volcanism, climate and erosion were responsible for structure of our present day earth ("James Hutton," 2002; Reimold, 2007, p. 8). Hutton is often referred to as the father of geology; he rejected catastrophism and, in its place, suggested a gradual change of the earth's crust over millions of years. Darwin was born in 1809, thirteen years after Hutton passed away. Darwin adapted Hutton's view of uniformitarianism, a view that continued to be advanced by a contemporary of Darwin, the Scottish geologist Sir Charles Lyell. Here is the modern definition of *Uniformitarianism*, from the *Columbia Electronic Encyclopedia*:

Uniformitarianism, in geology, doctrine holding that changes in the earth's surface that occurred in past geologic time are referable to the same causes as changes now being produced upon the earth's surface. ("Uniformitarianism," 2013)

Uniformitarianism was greatly advanced by Sir Charles Lyell (1797-1875); those that held to it clearly sought to extinguish the long-held tradition of catastrophism. Indeed, some scholars and philosophers saw catastrophism as a world view that brought scientific discovery in harmony with a traditional biblical world view. For example, the great flood of the Bible as described in the sixth chapter of Genesis, was a catastrophic event that was considered historically validated by scientific findings. However, for those who were ideologically opposed to science validating Bible passages, uniformitarianism was clearly unacceptable and therefore non-scientific because of its association with questions of metaphysics.

Sir Charles Lyell followed in the footsteps of Hutton by advancing the doctrine of catastrophism; Lyell simply carried out the task in a much more elegant manner which gained widespread acceptance in the scientific community. Charles Lyell proposed that the earth was formed by slow environmental changes that took place over a very long period of time. Lyell published his first edition of *Principles of Geology* (1830) and went on to publish 11 revisions. Lyell's views of uniformitarianism influenced Charles Darwin, who would later publish *On the Origin of Species* in 1859.

In the following passage Darwin speaks of his great affection for Sir Charles Lyell. Darwin had a copy of Lyell's first volume of *Principles of Geology* when he embarked on his voyage on the *Beagle* (Dec 1831 – Oct 1836)[17]. Ironically, Darwin was given Lyell's work by his Cambridge teacher and mentor, professor Henslow – who was not in agreement with Lyell's conclusions regarding uniformitarianism. Here, Darwin comments on his admiration of Sir Charles Lyell:

---

[17] (Barlow, 2005, p. 65)

The science of Geology is enormously indebted to Lyell –
more so, I believe, than any other man who ever lived. When
I was starting on the voyage of the Beagle, the sagacious
Henslow, who, like all other geologists believed at the time
in successive cataclysms, advised me to get and study the
first volume of the *Principles* [of Geology], which had just
been published ... (Barlow, 2005, p. 84)

The debate of catastrophism versus uniformitarianism or gradualism has been going on ever since Darwin published *On the Origin
of Species*. In a marvelous lecture delivered by geologist Clarence
King (1877) entitled "Catastrophism and Evolution," King maps
out the opposing scholarly views of catastrophism versus uniformitarianism. Clarence King led the U.S. geological exploration team
that surveyed the 40th parallel across Nevada, Utah, Colorado and
Wyoming; King became the founding director of the U.S. Geological
Survey in 1879. The lecture, "Catastrophism and Evolution," is a
marvelous tour de force on the subject and is a textbook example
of the sort of struggles that take place in the scientific community,
between contrasting scholarly viewpoints. This is precisely what
professor Thomas Kuhn (1962/1996) referred to as opposing paradigms in his classic work *The Structure of Scientific Revolutions*.

In King's lecture, he points out the long history of catastrophism on earth that existed prior to man and into recorded
history. According to King, accounts of catastrophism are recited by
Plutarch in his *Morals*, and are woven into the "Sanskrit, Hebrew,
and Mohammedan cosmogonies" (King, 1877, p. 451). In defense
of catastrophism, King cites the great French professor of zoology,
Georges Cuvier (1769-1832).

Science often swings like a pendulum, metaphorically as a
Kuhnsian[18] dance between opposing world views. We have mentioned that the dominant view of the history of the world was
catastrophism prior to the published work of geologists James
Hutton (1726-1797) and Sir Charles Lyell (1797-1875). Here is a
passage that refers to the once dominant catastrophic world view;

---

[18]   An homage to the professor of historical science, Thomas Kuhn (1962/1996).

it is published by the philosopher and evolution advocate Herbert Spencer (1891) who is quoting a lecture given by Professor Huxley:

> One-and-twenty years ago, in spite of the work commenced by Hutton and continued with rare skill and patience by Lyell, the dominant view of the past history of the earth was catastrophic. (p. 421)

The famous American geologist Clarence King recognized the significance of Lyell's uniformitarianism and its necessary adoption by Darwin in order to support Darwin's theories of descent with modification through natural selection. As King (1877) observed,

> It must be said, however, that biology, as a whole, denies catastrophism in order to save evolution. It is the common mistake of biologists to assume that catastrophes rest for their proof on breaks in the paleontological record meaning by that the observed gaps of life or the absence of connecting links of fossils between older and newer sets of successive strata. There never was a more serious error. Catastrophes are far more surely proved by the observed mechanical rupture, displacement, engulfment, crumpling, and crushing of the rocky surface of the globe. (pp. 463-464)

Finally, King suggests that the solution is to be found in neither of the classical definitions of catastrophism or uniformitarianism. Rather, King suggests that a solution exists as a synthesis between the two extremes. King proposes that since the argument is one of rapidity of energy transfer that the more accurate model would be that catastrophes are and have been the norm for millions of years. However, in using the term catastrophe this does not necessarily mean a worldwide devastation of all life on the planet whenever a catastrophic event occurs – it certainly could be in a portion of the planet as has been recorded in history and the geological record.

Such a proposition was later mirrored in biology more than a century later by the famous evolutionary biologist Stephen Jay Gould (2007), in his theory of punctuated equilibrium. Gould's theory proposed that the fossil record reflects long periods of stasis (stability) punctuated by occasional brief moments and sudden leaps in biological development. Although Gould's theory was not intended as either an admission or defense of catastrophism, it is not an unusual leap to suggest that there is a harmony between punctuated equilibrium and significant catastrophic world events.

Physicist Gerald Schroeder, who earned his Ph.D. at MIT observed, "A present look at the current theory of evolution reveals not a theory, but merely a description of the 'punctuated' jumps in the fossil record" (Schroeder, 2001, p. 91).

Geologists Coming out From Under the Rocks

Ever since the discovery of dinosaurs, a term meaning "terrible lizard" that was fashioned by the British anatomist Sir Richard Owen in 1842, geologists, paleontologists and biologists alike have been perplexed by the sudden disappearance of the dinosaurs from earth. The dinosaurs appeared about 230 million years ago and then suddenly disappeared about 65 million years ago. Prior to 1980, the explanation was that there were slow and natural changes in the climate that ultimately led to the demise of the dinosaurs. Part of the reason for the acceptance of the gradual decline theory was that uniformitarianism or gradualism was firmly established by Sir Charles Lyell and Charles Darwin, Spencer and Huxley. Herbert Spencer (1891) cites the following passage from a lecture by Professor Huxley in which Huxley discusses his disdain for those who support catastrophism along with his favorable view of uniformitarianism:

> The progress of scientific geology has elevated the fundament [sic] principle of uniformitarianism, that the explanation of the past is to be sought in the study of the present, into the position of an axiom; and the wild speculations of the catastrophists, to which we all listened with respect a quarter of a century ago, would hardly find a single patient hearer at the present day.

The great French zoologist Cuvier (1769-1832), defended catastrophism during his lifetime. But Cuvier was no longer alive when catastrophism fell out of favor, and uniformitarianism was established through the writings of geologist Sir Charles Lyell (1797-1875), and the great naturalist Charles Darwin (1809-1882). Darwin adopted Lyell's uniformitarian/gradualist hypothesis and based the theory of descent with modification upon the assumption of the doctrine of uniformitarianism. Prior to the 1980s, catastrophism was all but banned from the geology classrooms of the universities in the United States as scientific heresy!

Uniformitarianism in geology is referred to as gradualism by Darwin; the terms are for most practical purposes, synonymous. Darwin's theory of descent with modification hinges on a view of the world that gradually changes and is not suddenly impacted by catastrophic change. In the chapter titled "On the Geological Succession of Organic Beings" in *On the Origin of Species*, Darwin (1876/1998) asserts the notion that the theory of extinctions caused by catastrophic events is outdated and that the cause of extinctions has been replaced with a theory of gradual decline and eventual extinction of species:

> The old notion of all the inhabitants of the earth having been swept away by catastrophes at successive periods is very generally given up . . . On the contrary, we have every reason to believe, from the study of the tertiary formations, that species and groups of species gradually disappear. . . (pp. 449-450)

We have seen that human beings have witnessed catastrophic events for millennia and that the historical view of geological change was originally catastrophic. We have noted that the great geologists Hutton and Lyell advanced the idea of uniformitarianism, the idea that processes that operated in the past are no different than those that are observed now – in other words, geological change proceeds in a gradual manner. This is the idea that was embraced by Darwin and incorporated into Darwin's theory of descent with modification.

It was not until the 20th century that the dominant view of geology, uniformitarianism, began to be challenged.

Uniformitarianism and Gradualism Challenged

In the first half of the twentieth century, German paleontology professor Otto H. Schindewolf (1896-1971) dared to go against the dominant view of uniformitarianism by asserting a neo-cata-strophism, leading to mass extinction. Professor Schindewolf was boldly suggesting that mass extinctions that were evidenced in the fossil record (such as the dinosaurs 65 million years ago) were the result of catastrophe and not a gradual Darwinian process. In the 1950s, Schindewolf's ideas were not well received in the United States among geologists, paleontologists and biologists (Benton, 2003). Unfortunately, Schindewolf never lived to see his ideas vindicated among the worldwide scientific community.

Everything changed on June 6, 1980, when a remarkable paper was published in the scientific journal *Science*, by a team of researchers led by a physicist named Luis Alvarez (Luis W Alvarez, Alvarez, Asaro, & Michel, 1980). In that paper, Alvarez et al. claimed that they found evidence for the extinction of the dinosaurs 65 million years ago. The cause of the extinction was a catastrophic one; the researchers went out on a limb and claimed that they had discovered empirical evidence that suggested a spectacular meteor hit the earth approximately 65 million years ago and that this event impacted the entire planet, leading to the sudden extinction of the dinosaurs.

Luis Alvarez was a physicist and he assembled a team of researchers that included: geologist Walter Alvarez, and two staff scientists in the Energy and Environmental Division of Lawrence Berkely Laboratory; Frank Asaro and Helen Michel. Initially, the team was looking for a more accurate way to measure and validate the age of sedimentary evidence that marked the barriers between geological epochs. The team knew that the element of iridium is rare today on the earth's surface; they reasoned that an increased concentration of iridium would be evidence of older samples of the earth's sedimentary layers.

Alvarez (1980) and his team gathered evidence in clay samples retrieved from the Bottaccione George, near Gubbio, Italy; a second set of samples from the sea cliff of Stevns Klint, located 50 km south of Copenhagen, Denmark was also collected. What the researchers found was not what they expected. The researchers expected to see slow accumulations of iridium over time. Instead, the researchers were shocked to discover a sudden unaccounted for burst of iridium at the Cretaceous-Tertiary boundary (C/T); this was the period of time 65 million years ago, when the dinosaurs became extinct.

The team needed to confirm their findings, so they gathered samples from Denmark also. The Denmark samples confirmed the findings from Italy; both sets of samples showed an increase of iridium levels 65 million years ago at the C/T boundary. The researchers could not explain the high increase of iridium as a naturally occurring terrestrial event. Therefore, the Alvarez (1980) team made their shocking prediction to the scientific community:

> Impact of a large earth-crossing asteroid would inject about 60 times the object's mass into the atmosphere as pulverized rock; a fraction of this dust would stay in the stratosphere for several years and be distributed worldwide. The resulting darkness would suppress photosynthesis, and the expected biological consequences match quite closely the extinctions observed in the paleontological record. . . Four different independent estimates of the diameter of the asteroid give values that lie in the range 10 + (-) 4 kilometers. (p. 1095)

The effect of the Alvarez article in the 1980s is what Professor Kuhn (1962/1996) referred to as a scientific revolution. Uniformitarianism had been the reigning geological paradigm thanks to Lyell and Darwin. Now that paradigm was challenged with new scientific evidence. Over the next 20 years more research was done; it continued to support the hypothesis of the Alvarez team – earth had been hit by a giant asteroid 65 million years ago! The Alvarez et al. (1980) paper shook the current geological assumptions of the history of our planet to the core! Paleontologist, Michael Benton (2003) comments on the scientific revolution which resulted since 1980 in the fields of geology and the earth sciences:

> What a changed scientific world in 20 years! In 1980, despite the work of craterologists and the suggestion of a supernova explosion 65 million years ago, most earth scientists were still firmly in Charles Lyell's camp. When I learnt my geology in the 1970s, my professors did not even mention impacts, craters or mass extinctions. Now my students hear about catastrophes, asteroids, giant eruptions, death and destruction every week in their lectures. (p. 122)

Hundreds of scientific papers have been published since the Alvarez et al. article in 1980. As more research was conducted more craters were discovered on earth and an entirely new area of geology, studying "impact cratering" has now developed (Pälike, 2013; Reimold, 2003, 2007). An article by Urrutia-Fucugauchi and Perez-Cruz (2011) notes that between 170 and 180 impact craters have been identified on earth. There are certainly more since locating craters under the sea at the earth's poles is exceedingly difficult.

There were five known mass extinctions in the fossil record prior to 1980. However, these extinctions were minimized for almost one hundred years as the result of the doctrine of uniformitarianism. After the Alvarez team published their 1980 paper, the search was on for evidence of other massive craters that fit the time periods of the known mass extinctions in the geological record.

Alan Hildebrand, a Canadian graduate student along with other researchers reasoned that geological evidence pointed to a massive crater somewhere in the Caribbean. Hildebrand struck gold in Chicxulub Mexico when he and others located a massive crater buried underneath the earth and sea. The crater itself is no longer visible to the eye, nor evident from satellite photography; it was long buried by sediment and erosion over the last 65 million years.

In a brief paper published in *Science*, Heiko Pälike (2013) addressed the question of correlating a massive meteorite impact event with the mass extinction of the dinosaurs. Pälike independently confirmed the age of the Chicxulub Mexico crater as approximately 66 million years ago – a time period corresponding with the extinction of the dinosaurs.

Rebirth of Catastrophism

Catastrophism went out of favor with the writings of Hutton and Lyell and the ubiquitous acceptance of Darwin's theory of evolution (Anderson, 2007). But there are some geologists that prefer to look at the evidence left in stone – namely the earth itself. Michael Benton is a Professor of Vertebrate Paleontology and Head of the Department of Earth Sciences at the University of Bristol. Benton's (2003) book *When Life Nearly Died* is a modern day treatise to the concept of catastrophism. It is sound and scientific, and it is in no way written from a religious framework. Benton notes that in 1980 the scientific community was shaken with the discovery that there was evidence that a meteorite had collided with the earth 65 million years ago and that this historic event destroyed most of life on earth at the time, including the dinosaurs! The paleontologist Michael Benton (2003) summarizes the significance of this observation among the members of the scientific community:

> This marks one of the biggest shifts in scientific opinion of recent decades. From being regarded as pariahs, the *catastrophists* [sic.], geologists who point to larger-than-normal crisis in the geological past, have won the argument, in terms of extinctions of life in the past at least. In retrospect now, it is extraordinary to see how mainstream geologists denied the reality of catastrophes for so long. Their stance dates back to the 1830's, and early debates in geology which were won by the *uniformitarians* [sic.], scientists who argued that everything in the past could be explained by reference to modern slow-moving processes. (pp. 8-9)

The Greatest Catastrophe of All

While it is interesting that the mystery of the dinosaur's demise 65 millions of years ago may finally be solved, it is important to note that this was not the most significant mass extinction that occurred on earth. Geologists have identified five mass extinctions, in the earth's geological deposits. The greatest of these occurred at the end of the Permian period, 251 million years ago (Brand et al., 2012). The end-Permian extinction is credited with destroying 90-95% of all life on planet Earth! Scientists are still trying to explain how this took place. At this point, it does not appear that the cause was a meteor or some other extra-terrestrial source.

Professor of paleontology, Michael Benton (2003) suggests that the end-Permian extinction was caused by poisonous gas that was released from Siberia and was possibly accelerated by volcanic activity. The exact causes are not known but the evidence of extinction in the geological record is clear:

> The biggest mass extinction of all time did happen 251 million years ago, and even if we cannot yet fully explain why, it is important to look at the consequences of cutting life down to 10% or less of its normal diversity. (p. 283)

Apparently, Darwin was wrong. Natural selection was not the only driving force on earth that caused certain species to survive and others to become extinct. Mass extinctions did occur and scientists have confirmed five major catastrophic events in the geological record. Uniformitarianism is now out and catastrophism back in. The study of impact craters and the search for other causes of worldwide catastrophes causing mass extinctions is now a respectable topic of academic investigation.

Chapter Summary

Darwin proposed that natural selection was the necessary force behind his theory of descent with modification. Darwin knew that he needed a natural cause to explain the effect. Darwin argued that natural selection was the cause and that descent with modification was the effect.

We found that Darwin's theories were often improved upon by Herbert Spencer. Darwin proposed that natural selection was the cause of descent with modification. Spencer, in turn, modified the term natural selection and substituted his term "survival of the fittest." Darwin gave credit to Spencer's modification of terms in his sixth and final version of *On the Origin of Species* (1876).

The second part of the chapter discussed two competing forces of change upon the development of species. These two recent challengers to natural selection are evolutionary development and catastrophism.

Evolutionary development or Evo/Devo is asking questions about how multicellular beings develop from the embryo to the mature creature. This area of research has opened up because of advances in genetics, DNA research and microbiology. Paradoxically, Darwinism is both materialistic and reductionistic; it makes no room for metaphysical solutions. On the other hand, the development of the embryo is driven by coded information contained in the DNA of the living cell. DNA is information and thus is both incorporeal and metaphysical in nature. Therefore, the very existence of DNA, a material substance that contains information (a non-material code-of-life) is a paradox to the materialistic Darwinian paradigm.

Finally, we discussed a second threat to natural selection – catastrophism. Darwin was well aware of what catastrophism is. His disdain for catastrophism and support of Lyell's uniformitarianism are well documented in Darwin's publications and journal. Darwin's theory of descent with modification hinges on a gradual change of species over time. Catastrophism is antithetical to Darwin's theories because descent with modification postulated slow changes over time while catastrophism did not. Therefore, Darwin opposed catastrophism vehemently.

With the publication of the paper by Alvarez et al. (1980) everything changed. Alvarez and his research team demonstrated conclusively that a meteor had collided with the earth in the past and that this coincided with the extinction of the dinosaurs about 65 million years ago. Lyell and uniformitarianism are now out. Catastrophism is back in. Darwin and Lyell would be turning over in their final resting places if they were aware of the radical shift in earth science.

We now know that the earth has suffered five known mass extinctions; the largest one is called the end-Permian extinction. It wiped out 90-95 percent of all life on planet Earth. We think that we have a tremendous variety of life today, but in actuality we are the witnesses of the descendants of the 5–10 percent of living things that survived the end-Permian extinction (Benton, 2003). Apparently, Darwin was wrong, the earth had series of major catastrophes that effected the survival of every living creature; survival of the fittest is not the only force behind species changes over time.

An interesting side observation to mass extinctions being accepted in the scientific community is that the discussion has now begun to take on a political tone in the classroom. Some scientists are suggesting that we are entering a sixth mass extinction, one in which man is the cause (Barnosky et al., 2011; Wagler, 2011). Apparently, the stuff of Hollywood doomsday pictures is slowly becoming mainstream. This may be an interesting topic for the future.

This leads us to some questions about Darwinism and natural selection. Is neo-Darwinism at risk since natural selection is now being challenged by Evo/Devo theory and catastrophism? Will Stephen Gould's (2007) punctuated equilibrium theory gain strength as a sort of revised neo-Darwinsim? As one anthropologist said, "the only thing certain about culture is change." It appears that the cultural observation also applies to the scientific community.

III. Myth 3: Evolution is a Scientific Theory and a Fact

*Nothing in Biology Makes Sense Except in the
Light of Evolution*
Geneticist Theodosius Dobzhansky (1973)

*Because the evidence supporting it [biological evolution] is
so strong, scientists no longer question whether biological
evolution has occurred and is continuing to occur.*
**National Academy of Sciences and
Institute of Medicine** (2008, p.11)

D obzhansky's (1973) famous article "Nothing in Biology Makes Sense Except in the Light of Evolution," published in *American Biology Teacher* has been the reigning dictum for neo-Darwinists for decades. Dobzhansky's succinct statement summarized the neo-Darwinian paradigm. In other words, Dobzhansky put into words the world-view of most biologists, that evolution was a settled fact.

Most modern-day neo-Darwinists are convinced that evolution is a fact. Harvard University zoologist, Ernst Mayr refers to the "fact of evolution" (Mayr, 2001, p. 14). Famed evolutionary biologist Stephen Jay Gould proclaimed that "evolution is a theory. It is also a fact" (Gould, 1983, pp. 253-262). Professor of natural science, Ralph W. Lewis also argued that evolution is both a fact and a theory (Lewis, 1988). Biologist Douglas Futuyma is so convinced of the validity of evolution that he made the following statement: "the historical reality of evolution–is not a theory. It is a fact, as fully as the fact of the earth's revolution about the sun" (Futuyma, 1986, p. 15).

It is important to recognize what theories are. Theories are human constructions. Theories are not like rocks or bones that exist in the natural world. Theories cannot be measured in terms of size and weight; theories are ideas. Theories are created by humans to make sense out of data sets, that we call facts (Casmir, 1994). Theories can be modified or replaced completely, when new facts and new explanations for those facts are discovered. For Futuyma to suggest that evolution is a settled fact and to compare it to "the earth's revolution about the sun" is a gross misunderstanding of the scientific process. Theories have been falsified and then replaced throughout history and they will continue to be (Kuhn, 1962/1996). The example of the earth revolving around the sun is a case in point: for millennia, mankind believed that the sun and planets revolved around the earth.

What is a Scientific Theory?

We turn to the National Academy of Sciences (2008) for a definition of the term "science": "The use of evidence to construct testable explanations and predictions of natural phenomena, as well as the knowledge generated through this process" (p. 10).

Let's agree that the definition above is a workable operational definition for the term science. Does the term "evolution" fit the definition? I would argue that the term evolution does not fit the definition for science, stated above.

Once again here is Spencer's meaning of the term *evolution*:

As we now understand it, Evolution is definable as a change from an incoherent homogeneity to a coherent heterogeneity, accompanying the dissipation of motion and integration of matter" (Spencer, 1862/1898, p. 371).

Some may complain that I am using an 1898 definition of *evolution* for this discussion. They may also take issue with the fact that I am not using a more modern definition from current textbooks. I respond in the following manner: Darwin never proposed a theory called evolution; Darwin's theory was *descent with modification*. The entire reason that we use the term evolution today is that the philosopher Herbert Spencer argued for the use of the term *evolution* in his book: *First Principles* (Spencer, 1862/1898). If it were not for Herbert Spencer (1820–1903) and vigilant defenders of Darwin's theory (framed as evolution) such as biologist Thomas Huxley (1825-1895), we would probably not be debating the meaning of the term *evolution* today. Words enter into the common lexicon because they have utility in daily language; they are further promoted through academic publishing, education systems and the press.

Darwin did not accept Spencer's "Law of Evolution" as being either scientific in nature or useful in advancing knowledge. Darwin expressed his frustration with Spencer's deductive approach in the following statement:

Nevertheless I am not conscious of having profited in my own work by Spencer's writings. His deductive manner of treating every subject is wholly opposed to my frame of mind. His conclusions never convince me: and over and over again I have said to myself, after reading one of his discussions, - "Here would be a fine subject for half-a-dozen year's work." His fundamental generalizations (which have been compared in importance by some persons with Newton's Laws!) – which I daresay may be very valuable under a philosophical point of view, are of such a nature that they do not seem to me to be of any strictly scientific use. . . They do not aid one in predicting what will happen in any particular case. Anyhow they have not been of any use to me. (Barlow, 2005, p. 90)

Darwin makes several critical observations about Spencer's reasoning and use of the term evolution. First, Darwin disagrees with Spencer's deductive method of reasoning. Second, Darwin is insulted that Spencer's generalizations are compared to Newton's Laws. Third, Darwin prefers that Spencer's "fundamental observations" remain in the field of philosophy – and that they stay out of biology. Fourth (and most damning), Darwin clearly states that Spencer's method has no scientific usefulness and that it does "not aid in predicting what will happen in any particular case" (Barlow, 2005, p. 90).

In short, Darwin is stating that the term *evolution* is not scientific because it does not allow for prediction! Looking at the definition of "science" cited above by the National Academy of Sciences: "The use of evidence to construct testable explanations and predictions of natural phenomena . . ." Darwin is saying that Spencer's term "evolution" does help with making scientific predictions!

Did Darwin Discuss Falsifiability?

Darwin understood the importance of being able to disprove a theory if the facts and predictions made by the theory could not be supported. The idea of forming a methodology for scientific discovery was championed by Francis Bacon, something that Darwin was aware of when he wrote "I worked on Baconian principles . . ." (Barlow, 2005, p. 98). Chapter VI of *On the Origin of Species* is titled "Difficulties of the Theory." In that chapter, Darwin made the following statement:

> If it could be demonstrated that any complex organ existed, which could not possibly have been formed by numerous, successive, slight modifications, my theory would absolutely break down. But I can find no such case. (Darwin, 1876/1998, p. 232)

In the chapter that discusses "Difficulties of the Theory," Darwin included a section called "Organs of Extreme Perfection," in which he discusses the development of the eye. The eye is clearly a complex organ and Darwin was right to flag it as an "organ of perfection." As a researcher, Darwin saw the value of the Baconian method of scientific enquiry; Darwin raised an objection to his theory of descent with modification and then answered the criticism that he himself raised.

Space does not permit a complete discussion of Darwin's discourse on the eye. Darwin makes a fascinating comparison between the eye and a telescope, noting that humans have over time perfected the design of the telescope. Darwin makes a remarkable argument, "Have we any right to assume that the Creator works by intellectual powers like those of man? . . . May not believe that a living optical instrument might thus be formed as superior to one of glass, as the works of the Creator are to those of man?" (Darwin, 1876/1998, p. 231).

Darwin then explains that we use our "imagination" to consider transparent tissue filled with fluid that is light-sensitive. Further this transparent light-sensitive material is connected to a nerve that transfers the information to the brain. Darwin then suggests that natural selection renders a "power" that watches over this process yielding slight changes over millions of years to bring about the finished result. He then concludes the following: "May we not believe that a living optical instrument might thus be formed as superior to one of glass, as the works of the Creator are to those of man?" (Darwin, 1876/1998, p. 232). Darwin's conclusion is that the eye is superior to any man-made telescope. Darwin draws an analogy between a man-made optical instrument and a "living optical instrument" formed as "the works of the Creator." Darwin, thus breaks the current taboo in science; that one should not mix science with religion! Today, committed materialistic biologists would reject such an analogy in a heartbeat!

The eye argument continues to this day. The National Academy of Sciences (2008) argues that the eye could have been formed entirely from natural causes. They offer a series of five drawings suggesting the development of the eye by examining organs that are sensitive to light in living mollusks including the nautilus, murex and the octopus. The drawings are impressive, but the assumptions are severe. They suggest a teleological progression from one organism to the other over millions of years. None of this can be verified, because no one has observed each creature giving birth to another creature over millions of years, yielding the living creatures that we observe today. Thus, we are left with an excellent example of scientific narrative, without the corresponding facts to support the conclusions.

Like Darwin and the National Academy of Sciences, Oxford biologist Richard Dawkins also feels compelled to explain the development of the eye. Dawkins (1996) postulates, "Is there a continuous series of Xs connecting the modern eye to a state with no eye at all?" (p. 109). Dawkins answers his own question in the affirmative by suggesting that there has been an unbroken series of "imaginable Xs" (p. 109) that links a time when there was no eye, to a time when a functioning eye as we know it exists in human beings and other living creatures. Of course, this is bad science. Dawkins is submitting non-existing data, what he calls "imaginable Xs" to support his hypothesis. This is simply science at its worst. I do not think that Dawkins could go to a car dealership and pay for a new car with "imaginable money!"

Popper Criticizes Evolution

Philosopher Karl Popper (1982) pointed out that evolution is not a scientific theory: "Darwinism is not a testable scientific theory, but a *metaphysical research programme* – a possible framework for testable scientific theories" (p. 168).

Popper (1902-1994) is often quoted by those that seek to criticize or discredit evolution. The fact is, Popper (1982) liked the theory of evolution: "I have always been extremely interested in the theory of evolution, and very ready to accept evolution as a fact" (p. 167). Popper was intellectually honest; he admitted his bias towards accepting evolution. At the same time he devoted an entire chapter to trying to rescue evolution from its shortcomings. Chapter 37 of Popper's book, *Unended quest: an intellectual autobiography,* is titled "Darwinism as a Metaphysical Research Programme" (Popper, 1982).

1n 1961, Popper gave a Herbert Spencer Memorial Lecture. In that lecture, Popper tried to improve upon the idea of evolution, which he felt was scientifically weak. Darwin never approved of

Spencer's substitution of *descent with modification* with Spencer's term, *evolution*. Darwin criticized Spencer's methodology in the following manner: "His [referring to Herbert Spencer] deductive manner of treating every subject is wholly opposed to my frame of mind" (Barlow, 2005, p. 131). In other words, Darwin was opposed to Spencer's epistemology that used a broad based deductive treatment of facts to make grandiose statements about numerous "laws" that govern the universe.

Even though Popper did not read Darwin's autobiography, Popper's keen mind exposed the same problem with Spencer's treatment of descent with modification. In short, Spencer corrupted a scientific theory by applying deductive broad-stroked methodology to the question of origins. What Darwin called a "deductive manner of treating every subject," Popper called a *metaphysical research programme*. The result is the same, both are un-testable and therefore unscientific. In scientific terms, Spencer's theory of evolution is neither valid nor reliable. That is why Popper tried to improve upon evolution; he struggled to rescue it from certain doom. Popper's conclusion about the unscientific nature of evolution is without question:

> From this point of view the question of the scientific status of Darwinian theory – in the widest sense, the theory of trial and error-elimination – becomes an interesting one. I have come to the conclusion that Darwinism is not a testable scientific theory, but a metaphysical research programme [*sic*] – a possible framework for testable scientific theories. (Popper, 1982, p. 168)

Popper (1982) also observes, "I do not think that Darwinism can explain the origin of life. I think it quite possible that life is so extremely improbable that nothing can 'explain' why it originated" (p.169). As a philosopher, Popper gets to the root of the matter. Notice that he does not ponder "how" life originated; but rather, Popper asks "why?" The why question is clearly in the area of philosophy; it is outside of the realm of pure science. Science confines itself to natural laws and observations of naturally occurring phenomena. The why question suggests teleology, the purpose behind the phenomenon. Teleology assumes that there is progress over time to a higher or more advanced form of life. Darwin made a feeble attempt to address the teleological question when he stated: "And as natural selection works solely by and for the good of each being, all corporeal and mental endowments will tend to progress towards perfection" (Darwin, 1876/1998, p. 648).

This was an interesting hypothesis that Darwin set forth and yet there was no evidence produced to support it. First, what is perfection? How shall it be defined? How can evolution be marked as proceeding towards perfection? The arbitrary nature of the term *perfection* suggests that it defies a clear definition and therefore eludes any sort of declaration of achievement. Darwin's teleological explanation is therefore useful in any time period of life on earth, depending on how perfection is defined.

Popper (1982) saw this problem and once again tried to rescue the teleological theme:

> The theory sketched suggests something like a solution to the problem of how evolution leads towards what may be called "higher" forms of life. Darwinism as usually presented fails to give such an explanation. It can at best explain something like an improvement in the degree of adaptation. (p.176)

To summarize, Popper felt compelled to support evolution, since it was the prevailing paradigm of the academy. At the same time, Popper pointed out the weaknesses of evolution and its non-scientific methodology. Therefore, Popper attempted to improve upon evolution by devoting chapter 37 of Popper's book, *Unended quest: an intellectual autobiography* to the topic: "Darwinism as a Metaphysical Research Programme" (Popper, 1982). Whether Popper succeeded in strengthening neo-Darwinism is a question for other scholarly works.

We have seen that in the absence of directly observable evidence, specifically in the case of the development of the eye that Darwin (1859), the National Academy of Sciences (2008) and Richard Dawkins (1996) all used imagination to weave together a narrative that attempted to explain how the eye formed. We have also seen how the philosopher Karl Popper understood that for a hypothesis to be scientific, it also needs to be falsifiable. Popper faced the inherent problem with evolution – the fact that it is not falsifiable and thus concluded that evolution is "a metaphysical research programme [*sic*]" (Popper, 1982, p. 168).

While Popper is perhaps the most famous 20th century philosopher to challenge neo-Darwinism, 21st century philosopher Peter Williams (2017), has raised the question of 11 fallacies of evolutionary theory, by criticizing well known Neo-Darwinist, Richard Dawkins.

This discussion begs the question: If evolution is not the theory that Darwin had in mind when he proposed descent with modification, then what is exactly is evolution? Is the neo-Darwinism definition of evolution a scientific theory at all? I argue that what we call the *theory of evolution* today is not at all a scientific theory based on Baconian methods as Darwin originally proposed. Instead, I would suggest that what we call evolution is more of a narrative than a testable, valid and reliable scientific hypothesis.

Evolution - A Scientific Narrative

As a communication researcher, I would like to suggest that evolutionary research, as it exists today is based very little on observable data and more on a special form of rhetoric which language and rhetoric scholars Sheehan and Rode (1999) refer to as *scientific narrative*. In their article "On Scientific Narrative: Stories of Light by Newton and Einstein," Sheehan and Rode (1999) suggest that narrative and scientific discourse can be complimentary. They analyze texts from both Isaac Newton and Albert Einstein to support their thesis.

I do not disagree that narrative aids the reader in understanding difficult, abstract and sometimes metaphysical concepts. Indeed, both Newton and Einstein were dealing with physics and forces that could be measured but not seen. This becomes an ontological question, a question about what is real.

I would like to suggest that Sheehan and Rodes' concept of scientific narrative has merit and is suitable for expansion. *Narrative* is a type of storytelling; it is both a story and an account of events. Narrative can be both fictional and factual. When we talk about fictional narrative, we refer to works of fiction such as novels, plays, and motion pictures. Of course, novels, plays and motion pictures can also be based on historical facts.

From the scientific perspective, narrative attempts to answer the why question. For example, when looking at a scientific paper the organization of the paper follows a standard style: introduction, literature review, methodology, results, and discussion. The introduction sets the stage for the reason of the inquiry. The literature review looks at the current state of knowledge on the topic. The methodology describes how the research will be done in detail and how the data will be gathered. The results consist of the data that are gathered and the presentation of that data in graphs, charts or statistical analysis. Finally, the discussion is the interpretation of the data. The discussion wrestles with the difficult why questions: it is a special type of scientific narrative that explains what the data mean and what the implications are.

Evolution unfortunately does not follow the standard pattern of scientific scholarship, outlined above. Evolutionary inquiry often breaks from the other scientific research because narratives are substituted for data. This is problematic, since a narrative is subjective; a narrative explaining past events is not a measurable independently observable piece of evidence. In other words, prehistoric events are interpreted and presented as a narrative from an evolutionary world view. The scientific narrative data are then used as evidence to support the theory of evolution. This is circular reasoning, or what philosophers call a tautology.

Evolution commits the fallacy of substituting a scientific narrative in the place of actual empirical data. The fallacy is further compounded by the fact that narrative substituted for empirical evidence is not necessarily valid or reliable. Validity and reliability are cornerstones of the scientific method. Let's take a look at some text to see how narrative is substituted for empirical data.

Here is a curious comment about the eye from Darwin, "how a nerve comes to be sensitive to light, hardly concerns us more than how life itself originated" (1876/1998, p. 228). Darwin is saying, it's not important to talk about how a nerve became sensitive to light, it's just as unimportant as discussing how life first began on earth![19] Many scholars since Darwin have attempted to address the gap that Darwin left: the inability to explain the formation of the eye and the origin of life itself. Darwin (1876/1998) continues his discussion of the eye and substitutes belief, for direct scientific observation.

> Let this process go on for millions of years; and during each year on millions of individuals of many kinds; and may we not **believe** [emphasis added] that a living optical instrument might thus be formed as superior to one of glass . . .? (p. 232)

Once again, this is just bad science, because belief is not evidence! Invoking belief as evidence to support a scientific conclusion is poor methodology at best.

Richard Dawkins (1996) invokes abstract reasoning and imagination as evidence of the formation of the eye [bold emphasis added below]:

> So far, by a process of more-or-less **abstract reasoning**, we have concluded that there is a series of **imaginable Xs**, each sufficiently similar to its neighbors that it could **plausibly** turn into one of its neighbors, the whole series linking the human eye back to no eye at all. (p. 109)

Here is the pattern. Darwin evokes **belief** in change over millions of years, while Dawkins suggests that **abstract reasoning**, **imaginable Xs** and **plausibility** can be used as evidence! Once again, we see narrative and storytelling being used as substitutes for empirical data. In short, the narrative has become both data and

---

[19] It is important to note that in Darwin's book *The Origin of Species,* Darwin did not present any theory to explain how the first living creature appeared on Earth. This will be discussed in further detail in the next chapter.

the explanation for the data. As Popper concluded, evolution is a "metaphysical research programme [*sic*]." Belief and imagination are metaphysical concepts. Belief and imagination are not empirical data; they are not valid and reliable facts. We turn now to one of the cornerstones of evolutionary theory, homology. Homology began as comparative anatomy between similar organisms in the early 1800s (Prothero, 2007a, p. 105). Ernst Mayr defines *homologous* as: "Referring to the structure, behavior, or other character of two taxa that is derived from the same or equivalent feature of their nearest common ancestor" (Mayr, 2001, p. 287).

The Narrative of Homology

Much of the evidence for evolution does not come from direct observation at all; it comes from assumptions and narratives. For example, the term homology refers to a similarity in structure between different species. Homology has been used as evidence for descent with modification, or what is now called evolution. Geologist Donald Prothero (2007a) discusses homology in the following manner:

> The basic vertebrate forelimb (fig. 4.8) has the same basic elements: a single large bone (the humerus), a pair of two long bones in the forearm (the radius and ulna), a number of wrist bones (carpals and metacarpals), and multiple bones (phalanges) supporting five digits (fingers). But look at the wide array of ways that some animals use this basic body plan! Whales have modified them into a flipper, while bats have extended the fingers out to support a wing membrane. Birds also developed a wing, but in an entirely different way, with most of the hand and wrist bones reduced or fused together, and feather shafts . . . None of this makes any sense unless these animals inherited a standard body plan in place from their distant ancestors and had to modify it to suit their present-day function and ecology. (pp. 105-106)

Prothero's description of homology in the structure of the fore-limb or hand is used as evidence for evolution. Look closely at the passage above; it is not a series of testable scientific observations that lead to supporting a theory. These are many observations that have been woven together into a story. Homology is a narrative; it is a notion that there was a common ancestor that ties these creatures together. The problem is, no one has observed the unnumbered ancestors giving birth over a period of unspecified time to arrive at the present. The hypothesis is completely untestable! Evolutionary biologist Ernst Mayr (2001) was intellectually honest when he points out that "homology cannot be proven; it is always inferred" (p. 27).

Evolution is a narrative; it is a story with a beginning, a struggle for existence, and a present-day reality. It is an exciting story – but narrative and inference are weak substitutes for empirical scientific methodology! We turn now to phylogeny, depicted in the drawing of a tree that shows the evolution of all living things over time.

The Narrative of Phylogeny

Phylogeny is more commonly referred to as "the tree of life." In essence, phylogeny is homology on a much grander scale, it is the linking together of all homologous organisms from the beginning of life to the present! Darwin only had one illustration in his entire book. Figure 1, is Darwin's illustration which shows his theory that present-day life may have come from one or a few first life forms (Darwin, 1876/1998, p. 149). Darwin's hypothesis is that all living things that are observed today are direct descendants of earlier life forms "originally breathed by the Creator into a few forms or into one" (Darwin, 1876/1998, p. 649). Darwin was saying that he did not know if all of life began from one living thing or possibly two living things, that both began at about the same time in the past and that the cause of life was the "Creator." In Darwin's drawing, he illustrates the idea that all of life began from two single-celled life forms.[20]

---

[20]   Darwin also asserts that the "laws impressed on matter" were done so by "the Creator" (Darwin, 1876/1998, p. 647).

Today, we lack certainty about how life began, because no human being was there to observe the moment when life began on Earth!

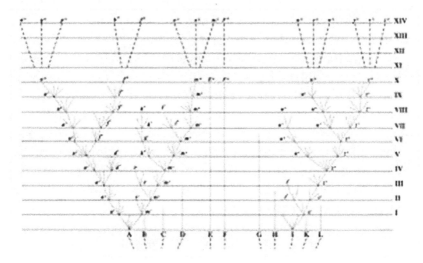

Figure 1 Darwin's Diagram of the First Life Forms on Earth

Here is evolutionary biologist Ernst Mayr's (2001) definition of *phylogeny*: "The inferred lines of descent of a group of organisms, including a reconstruction of the common ancestor and the amount of divergence of the various branches" (p. 289).[21] There are two important points here; first, the definition states that phylogeny is inferred. This means that like homology it is assumed. Of course, different observers can assume different things. Therefore, phylogeny is also a "metaphysical research programme [*sic*]" (Popper, 1982, p. 168). Second, a comparison of biology textbooks will quickly reveal that biologists do not agree on phylogeny. Diversity of life diagrams are drawn hundreds of different ways in hundreds of different textbooks and articles.

Phylogeny is another example of a narrative; it tells a story in a picture form. The story is based on inference and not on direct

---

[21] Mayr (1999) also wrote, *Systematics and the origin of species, from the viewpoint of a zoologist*. Systematics studies the diversity of organisms. It incorporates taxonomy, phylogeny and biodiversity.

observable facts – branches of the tree can be drawn wherever the artist chooses. I agree with Charles Darwin who criticized Spencer's term *evolution,* by stating that it does "not aid one in predicting what will happen in any particular case" (Barlow, 2005, p. 90). When it comes to prediction, phylogeny could be compared to drawing the bull's eye around arrows that hit the side of a blank wall. The arrows are the data, and the phylogeny tree diagram is the bull's eye that is drawn around the data to support the hypothesis. We now turn away from the problem of phylogeny to a more pressing question: Can evolution be both a theory and a fact?

Is Evolution a Fact?

Many biologists, geologists, and scientists state that evolution is a fact. Biologist, Ernst Mayr (2001) in *What Evolution Is*, refers to the 'fact of evolution" (p. 14). By stating that evolution is a fact, the conversation becomes dead-ended. In other words, if one believes that something is true, then there is very little to add to the observation. The problem with the entire discussion of whether evolution is a theory, or a fact is that this is the premise is false. There is a clear logical inconsistency here. Facts are data; theories make sense out of facts.

Following the Baconian method of scientific discovery, facts are observed instances of natural phenomena. One fact is a datum. Many facts are data (the plural form of datum). Facts therefore represent empirical data. In contrast, theories are not data at all: Theories are explanations for data. Theories try to make sense out of empirical facts. An explanation cannot be data; data cannot be an explanation. Following this logic, evolution cannot be a fact, since a theory cannot be a fact. Again, theories are explanations for facts – but they are not facts themselves. To suggest that evolution is a fact is to commit a serious scientific fallacy of logic.

Data that are gathered properly are verifiable by other researchers. We say that the data are valid and reliable. Valid data are data that reflect an accurate measure of the phenomena being studied. Reliable data are data that can be observed again by other researchers – yielding similar results while controlling variables.

There is very little meaning in a single datum, or observation. However, when a data set is studied at the macro level – that is when meaning may begin to emerge. Theories provide the explanatory power to make sense out of data sets. Using the scientific method, it is precisely this ability to explain patterns in nature that make theories so useful! In other words, theories help to make sense out of the natural world that surrounds us.

Here is a way to picture the relationship between a datum, data, and theories. Remember, a datum is a fact – a single observation. The diagram is best viewed from the bottom, to the top.

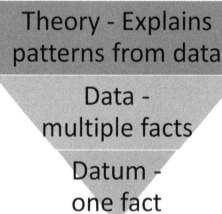

Figure 2 The Inductive Method of Scientific Research

Figure 2 is a visual representation of the scientific method, or inductive reasoning. Inductive reasoning gathers specific facts (observations) and then looks for patterns. When patterns emerge, theories can be formed to explain the patterns. Researchers refer to this as generalizability. In other words, can the patterns which represent some sample of a population be generalized to the larger, general population? Following are two observations about the construction of scientific theories.

First, the scientific method is an inductive bottom-up approach. It uses facts gathered from a selected population, and works its way from the bottom-up, towards theory construction. As you can see, it makes no sense to call a theory a fact! This is a complete misuse of terminology. Theories are never facts. Facts are never theories. In the scientific method, facts are gathered to help construct theories.

Second, scientific theories are human constructions. Theories do not exist naturally. Theories are inherently metaphysical since theories are ideas. Ideas cannot be observed naturally in nature – since ideas are incorporeal. Ideas are human constructions of the mind.

Therefore, evolution cannot be a fact. Evolution was a theory that was constructed primarily in the mind of Herbert Spencer. Descent with modification and natural selection are theories that were constructed in the mind of Charles Darwin. Theories cannot be found on a tree or under a rock somewhere. They can only be found in a human mind. Of course, theories can be published in written form, as in *On the Origin of Species* (Darwin, 1876/1998).

In conclusion, when it comes to the construction of scientific theories, scientists say that theories are either supported or not supported. If a theory is supported, then it is understood that the facts gathered present enough evidence to support the theory. In contrast, if the facts gathered do not present enough evidence to support the theory, then the theory needs to be either modified or rejected in favor of a new theory. This has been the scientific process for hundreds of years.

Chapter Summary

This chapter addressed the myth that evolution is both a scientific theory and a fact. The myth was necessary to discuss because well-known Darwinists such as zoologist Ernst Mayr (2001, p. 14), and biologist Douglas Futuyma (1986, p. 15) proclaimed that evolution is both a theory and a fact. Archaeologist Cameron M. Smith (2011) is so convinced that the theory of evolution is a fact, that he wrote a book titled: *The Fact of Evolution*.

In this chapter, we have looked at the definitions and the application of both theories and facts to scientific understanding. We learned that theories are created by human beings in order to interpret and make sense of the world around us. In this sense, a theory gives a framework or a lens to look at a data set (a group of facts) to make sense out the observations. We also learned that scientific theories are special kinds of theories. Scientific theories allow for the prediction of future observations. Darwin's original theory, which appeared in the first five versions of *On the Origin of Species*, was called descent with modification. In the sixth and final edition of *On the Origin of Species*, Darwin adopted Herbert Spencer's term, evolution. Darwin was highly critical of Spencer's methodology and term *evolution*. Darwin criticized Spencerian evolution when he stated that evolution does "not aid one in predicting what will happen in any particular case" (Barlow, 2005, p. 90).

Darwin understood that for a theory to be regarded as robust and scientific, it must stand up to both criticism and the possibility of falsifiability. Therefore, Darwin included an entire chapter on "Difficulties of the Theory." Darwin supposed correctly that certain organs would pose a problem for his theory of natural selection. Therefore, Darwin attempted to explain how the eye (which Darwin called an "organ of perfection") could be the result of natural selection. Darwin's explanation of how the eye could result from natural selection is weak. Darwin mixes science with religion by concluding: "May we not believe that a living optical instrument might thus be formed as superior to one of glass, as the works of the Creator are to those of man?" (Darwin, 1876/1998, p. 232).

More than one hundred years later, the National Academy of Sciences (2008) struggles to explain the existence of the eye by showing drawings of eyes in living creatures that are in various forms of development. The weakness in this example is that there is no way to know that the human eye progressed through these various stages; there are no direct observations of the progress over millions of years; there is only inference.

Biologist Richard Dawkins also attempts to rescue the explanation of the development of the eye from harsh criticism by inventing data that do not exist! Dawkins (1996) postulates, "Is there a continuous series of Xs connecting the modern eye to a state with no eye at all?" (p. 109). The response to the question is rhetorical since it cannot be demonstrated as either true or false. Thus, we are left with the conclusion of philosopher Karl Popper.

Philosopher of science Karl Popper (1902-1994) argued that evolution is a "metaphysical research programme [*sic*]" (Popper, 1982, p. 168). Popper supported the overall notion of evolution. At the same time, Popper saw weaknesses in the theory and tried to repair them in chapter 37 of his book, *Unended quest: an intellectual autobiography*. Chapter 37 is titled: "Darwinism as a Metaphysical Research Programme [*sic*]" (Popper, 1982). Popper also felt that Darwinism would be overreaching if it was applied to the origin of life itself. Popper (1982) concluded, "I do not think that Darwinism can explain the origin of life. I think it quite possible that life is so extremely improbable that nothing can 'explain' why it originated" (p.169).

In this chapter, I argued that evolution is not a scientific theory, but that it is rather a narrative. I discussed how narrative is commonly used in scientific literature as an explanation for observed data. Conversely, it is tautological for narrative to be substituted as data, to later be interpreted as evidence to support a theory. This tautological problem with Darwinian texts is a glaring weakness in neo-Darwinian dogma, since the narrative that is substituted for data is often neither valid nor reliable.

This weakness can be further demonstrated in the concepts of homology and phylogeny. Homology is a narrative; it is a romantic notion that there was a common ancestor that ties these creatures with similar structures together – as being descendants from one another or some other common ancestor. The metaphysical nature of homology is evident in that it can neither be proven or disproven. Evolutionary biologist Ernst Mayr (2001) is intellectually honest when he points out that "homology cannot be proven; it is always inferred" (p. 27).

Similarly, phylogeny, or what we more commonly refer to as *the tree of life* is also a metaphysical concept; a concept that can be neither proven nor disproven. Similar to homology, biologist Ernst Mayr (2001) points out that phylogeny is also an inferred concept:

87

"The inferred lines of descent of a group of organisms, including a reconstruction of the common ancestor and the amount of divergence of the various branches" (p. 289). In Mayr's definition, phylogeny is inferred, it is therefore metaphysical and can neither be proven nor disproven. Both homology and phylogeny are inferred; they both are metaphysical narratives that defy empirical observation.

Finally, there is the question, "Is evolution a fact?" The scientific process is an inductive one. It begins with a collection of empirical data and then tries to make sense out of those data through a process of theory-making. Theories are constructed by humans in order to make sense out of the world around us. Theories are either supported or not supported, based on the analysis of the data. It is circumvention of the scientific method to propose that a theory can simultaneously be both a fact and a theory. It is logically inconsistent for theories which are human constructions to be considered as facts, since facts are empirical natural phenomena. In contrast, theories are not natural; theories are a product of mind. Since empirical data are a product of the natural world; theories and facts cannot be equivalent.

In conclusion, for any professor, author or researcher to stand before a class of secondary or undergraduate students and declare that evolution is a fact, is to only display a commitment to Darwinian dogma. A true scientist, researcher, or scholar who agrees with neo-Darwinism should rather proclaim that they feel the evidence supports the theory. There is perhaps no other subject more hotly contested regarding adherents to neo-Darwinism and its critics. The National Academy of Science (2008) continues to argue that evolution is a fact. This is precisely why they published the book: *Science, Evolution, and Creationism.*

Because the evidence supporting it is so strong, scientists no longer question whether biological evolution has occurred and is continuing to occur. Instead, they investigate the mechanisms of evolution, how rapidly evolution can take place, and related questions. (p. 11)

The statement that "scientists no longer question whether biological evolution has occurred" is inaccurate. This book is full of citations from scientists who question biological evolution! The next chapter details how evolutionary theory has absolutely no explanation for how life itself formed on Earth. Charles Darwin himself had no explanation for how life began on Earth. If evolution cannot explain how life began in the first place, then the entire theory collapses and must be reevaluated.

IV. Myth 4: Evolution Explains the Origin of Life

*Our ignorance is as profound on the origin of life
as on the origin of force on matter.*
Naturalist Charles Darwin (1863a)

*Because the earliest fossils are tiny carbonized films
preserved in cherts [sic] and flints, they provide little
evidence for the chemical processes that formed life.*
Geologist Donald R. Prothero (2007a, p. 147)

In the classroom, students are repeatedly given the impression that
evolution explains both the origin of life and the varieties of life
that exist today. Even if students in grades K-12 do not hear the following: "Evolution explains the appearance of the first living cell on
earth," they will conclude the same in the absence of any competing
theory. Students are very impressionable and easily persuaded by
teachers and subject matter experts. In general, it is not in the nature
of most young children to challenge an adult in a classroom and
ask for empirical evidence when a theory is being presented. Such
critical thinking skills are often encouraged at the senior high school
and college levels.

How is the idea that evolution explains the origin of life prop-
agated in our public schools? It is done subtly; organizations such
as the National Science Teachers Association (NSTA) oppose any

criticism of evolution or alternative theories. The following statement was adopted by the NSTA Board of Directors, July 2003:

> Science textbooks should emphasize evolution as a unifying concept. Publishers should not be required or volunteer to include disclaimers in textbooks that distort or misrepresent the methodology of science and the current body of knowledge concerning the nature and study of evolution. (NSTA, 2013)

The passage above appears in a document called, "NSTA Position Statement: The Teaching of Evolution." The NSTA began in 1944 and claims a current membership of greater than 55,000 educators, administrators and science professionals. It is no understatement to say that the NSTA has a strong influence on how the topic of science is taught in public schools. It also has influence upon school boards and publishers. The NSTA clearly only wants evolution to be taught in the public schools; it advocates the exclusion of any criticism of evolution from the scientific community. The NSTA also forbids the introduction of any competing theories to be published in K-12 textbooks. This is quite fascinating in a nation that restricts Congress, in the First Amendment of the U.S. Constitution, from passing a law that abridges "the freedom of speech". Apparently, the NSTA has no problem limiting free speech, in written form, if it runs contrary to their view of the theory of evolution!

The National Education Association (NEA) is a very powerful union representing three million K-12 teachers and administrators; it is also the largest public employee union in the United States. The NEA has a web page called: "Understanding Evolution."[22] The page has links to the evolution.berkely.edu web site. On that site, there is a discussion called "Misconceptions about Evolution." The text below (from the website) is quite confusing. It suggests that the statement "evolution is a theory about the origin of life" is a misconception and therefore not valid. However, the correction contradicts

---

[22] NEA webpage called, "Understanding Evolution" (http://www.nea.org/tools/lessons/55490.htm)

the misconception by stating that evolution "does encompass ideas and evidence regarding life's origins." This is clearly contradictory rhetoric.

MISCONCEPTION: Evolution is a theory about the origin of life.

CORRECTION: Evolutionary theory *does* encompass ideas and evidence regarding life's origins (e.g., whether or not it happened near a deep-sea vent, which organic molecules came first, etc.), but this is not the central focus of evolutionary theory. Most of evolutionary biology deals with how life changed *after* its origin. Regardless of how life started, afterwards it branched and diversified, and most studies of evolution are focused on those processes. ("Misconceptions about Evolution," 2012)

Often, what is taught in public schools and what is believed by the public are two different things. In the case of evolutionary biology and the origin of life, there are some striking differences between textbook material and public opinion.

What does the Public think about Life's Origins?

What does the public think about the origin of life? In a 2006, Gallup Poll released aggregate data from multiple polls taken by Gallop between 2001 and 2005. Here are the results: only 12% of Americans believe that human beings had an origin that developed without God's help. This contrasts with 36% that believe God helped to develop human beings from less advanced forms and 47% of Americans that believe God created humans in their present form. Also, from the same Gallup study, it is interesting to note that the more educated a person becomes, the less likely he or she is to believe that God created human beings in their present form. The survey shows that 58% of people with a high school degree (or less) agreed that "God created human beings in present form" (Gallup,

2006). The percentage of agreement to the statement decreases with more education.

- 48% with some college agree to the statement
- 38% with college degrees agree to the statement
- 25% with postgraduate education agree to the statement

In statistics, this is called an inverse relationship: When one variable goes up, the other goes down. In this poll, we see that as years of education increase from high school to postgraduate studies, the belief that "God created human beings in present form" drops from 58% to 25%.

These findings are not surprising since students tend to emulate their professors. The longer students are in school, the more likely they are to think like their professors think. There is a highly significant difference of opinion between the academic community and the public about the origin of life. In a poll conducted by the Pew Research Center, it was found that 87% of scientists believe that humans and other living things have evolved over time due to natural processes (Kohut, 2009, p. 37). In contrast, only 32% of the public believe that humans and other living things have evolved over time due to natural processes.

Even though Darwin's theory of descent with modification (evolution) was not meant to address the origin of life itself, evolutionary biologists and public education unions such as the National Education Association seek to advance a materialistic[23] view of creation.

What the Gallup Poll data show, is that the public does not seem to agree with the scientific community. Only 32% of the public versus 87% of the scientific community agree with the statement that "humans and other living things have evolved over time due to natural processes." In addition, the Gallop data show that when a person studies at the university and moves on to graduate school, that person is more likely to agree with the statement that "humans and other living things have evolved over time due to natural processes."

---

[23]   *Materialism* – a philosophical doctrine that advances the notion that nothing exists except matter which is understood by certain natural laws of physics.

It should be no surprise that the longer a person remains and studies in higher education, the more likely that person will hold a world view like that of his/her professors.

What can we gather by these findings? Modern educators and large public-school unions such as the National Education Association and the National Science Teachers Association are committed to teaching evolution as a theory that explains both the development and the origin of life itself. We also learned that most of the American public does not agree that evolution explains the beginning of life on this planet.

We turn now to the question of what Darwin believed about the origin of life. Didn't Darwin believe that descent with modification also explained how life itself began? Wasn't it Darwin himself that wrote to a friend and suggested that life could have begun in a warm little pond somewhere on earth, millions of years ago?

Darwin's Warm Little Pond

Darwin wrote a letter to his friend and research assistant, botanist Joseph D. Hooker in 1871, speculating that life could have begun in some "warm little pond" millions of years ago (Darwin, 1871). The letter has become quite famous and it is often cited as a hypothesis of how life could have begun on earth:

> But if (and oh what a big if) we could conceive in some warm little pond with all sort of ammonia and phosphoric salts,—light, heat, electricity present, that a protein compound was chemically formed, ready to undergo still more complex changes, at the present such matter would be instantly devoured, or absorbed, which would not have been the case before living creatures were formed (Pereto, Bada, & Lazcano, 2009)

Scholars and students of history must be very careful not to read too much into Darwin's 1871 letter to Joseph Hooker. Extreme caution must be taken in the interpretation of the letter from Darwin to Hooker. The letter is neither a published scientific theory nor an acknowledgement of spontaneous generation. The private letter is merely a correspondence from one scholar to another.

Eight years prior to Darwin's "warm little pond" letter to Hooker, Darwin wrote a public letter that was published in *Athenaeum. Journal of Literature, Science, and the Fine Arts*. In that letter, Darwin penned his sharp disagreement with the doctrine of spontaneous generation:

> A mass of mud with matter decaying and undergoing complex chemical changes is a fine hiding-place for obscurity of ideas . . . Now is there a fact, or a shadow of a fact, supporting the belief that these elements, without the presence of any organic compounds, and acted on only by known forces, could produce a living creature? At present it is to us a result absolutely inconceivable. (Darwin, 1863b)

Unfortunately, our modern education system is selective in its telling of scientific history and discovery. Darwin's "warm little pond" letter is often quoted by educators. However, the telling of history is not balanced by Darwin's disdain of the idea of spontaneous generation – for lack of evidence. It is important to note that in the 1871 letter to Hooker, Darwin gives no evidence for spontaneous generation. Darwin is only posing an unsupported "what if" scenario to a friend; Darwin is not suggesting a formal scientific hypothesis. Nevertheless, the popular myth of Darwin's "warm little pond" continues to this day. Follmann and Brownson at the Institute of Biology, University of Kassel published an article in which they refer to Darwin's "warm little pond" and then they suggest that "complex organic matter could have formed spontaneously on pristine planet Earth about 4,000 mya [million years ago]" (Follmann & Brownson, 2009).

Recently, a group of professors from Iowa State University wrote the following in the journal of *Evolution: Education and Outreach*:

> The propagation of misconceptions about the theory of biological evolution must be addressed whenever and wherever they are encountered. . . including: that biological evolution

explains the origin of life . . . (Clough, Colbert, Kelly, Rice, & Warner, 2010)

These are professional educators who are saying that Darwin's theory does *not* explain the origin of life! It is more common today that high school science teachers suggest to students that the formation of life on earth was an entirely materialistic process – a process explained by evolution.

Darwin did not claim that his theory of natural selection explained the beginning of life. Darwin's theory proposed that natural selection is the driving force behind change. Darwin suggested that through mutation certain organisms would survive, while organisms less suitable to the environment would eventually perish. This is a plausible explanation for the existence of living things today. However, natural selection and genetic mutation are not part of the equation when we are discussing the beginning of life itself. In short, if there is no life, there can be no process of natural selection or mutation. Natural selection and mutation only occur after life begins; they offer no explanation whatsoever of the first living cell.

In the following passage Darwin states that the data are insufficient to arrive at any conclusion about how life on earth began. He also criticizes Herbert Spencer in his universal application of the term evolution:

Looking to the first dawn of life, when all organic beings, as we may believe, presented the simplest structure, how, it has been asked, could the first steps in the advancement or differentiation of parts have arisen? Mr. Herbert Spencer would probably answer that, as soon as simple unicellular organisms came by growth or division to be compounded of several cells, or became attached to any supporting surface, his law "that homologous units of any order become differentiated in proportion as the relations to incident forces become different" would come into action. But as we have no facts to guide us, speculation on the subject is almost useless. (Darwin, 1876/1998, p. 164)

In the passage above, Darwin makes it clear that, "we have no facts to guide us" (Darwin, 1876/1998, p. 164). The situation has not changed today. Today, scientists and educators continue to have no facts to guide them about the first living cell on earth. No one was there at the time to take notes. In addition, the spontaneous generation of life is not occurring anywhere today. No one has ever observed life coming from non-life. But wait. Didn't Miller and Urey create life in a test tube in 1953?

Miller and Urey and the Building Blocks of Life

Stanley Miller and Harold Urey thought they explained the beginning of life by forming a few amino acids in a laboratory. But a few amino acids are not the same thing as a living cell. In the original Miller and Urey experiment (which synthesized four amino acids in a laboratory) scientists selected carbon dioxide, water, nitrogen, ammonia, and methane and then introduced electricity (Berra, 1990). In other words, the scientists selected ingredients and conditions that would produce the desired results. This is similar to Thomas Edison who intentionally set out to create the light bulb. After hundreds of trials and over a year of research, Edison discovered a carbon thread filament that produced light! No one would make an argument that light bulbs popped up spontaneously out of the earth.

In like fashion, Miller and Urey, in their 1953 experiment, set out to create amino acids and they succeeded in creating four– however it took the *intelligence* of Miller and Urey to do it! Miller and Urey intentionally set up conditions that would yield a favorable result. But let's just give Miller and Urey the credit for trying to recreate the conditions on planet Earth 3.5 billion years ago that *may* have existed. Let's assume that the assumptions of Miller and Urey were correct and that the early earth atmosphere was created accurately in the experiment (which is a big assumption since no one was there). There are two major problems with the resulting four amino acids that were produced from the experiment.

First, the formation of four amino acids from the Miller and Urey experiment is not very impressive. Simple proteins are built from

20 amino acids (Barron, 2008; Crick, 1981, p. 44). The Miller and Urey experiment did not yield the necessary 20 amino acids to build a protein. Microbiologists compare the 20 amino acids to letters in an alphabet. An experiment that yields four letters in a 20-letter alphabet is not a success. For example, the English language has 26 letters. Imagine how difficult it would be to read and write English if your first-grade teacher limited you to only four letters!

Second, the amino acids that were created in the Miller and Urey experiment were not all capable of producing life. Amino acids have the peculiar property of being left or right handed. Curiously, amino acids found in almost all living things (except diseased tissue) are always left handed. Scientists have struggled to explain why life prefers to be left-handed. Left and right handed amino acids cannot combine together to form a protein (Crick, 1981).The concept of handedness in molecules is known as *chirality* (Barron, 2007, 2008). The curious thing about life is that, all living things have exhibit left-handed chirality known as *homochirality* (Klabunovskii, 2012). Molecular biologists, chemists and other researchers have so much to say about the topic of chirality that there is a scientific journal devoted entirely to this topic, the scientific journal: *Chirality*. Figure 3 shows representations of left and right-handed amino acid molecules. Like left and right-handed gardening gloves, amino acid molecules are also handed, or chiral; they are mirror images of each other. For example, if you try to put a left-handed glove on your right hand it won't fit.

Figure 3 Left and Right-Handed Amino Acid Molecules

Apparently, there exists no evolutionary reason or explanation for the fact that all life exhibits homochirality. The puzzling reality is that all of life seems to be biased and homochiral; no one can explain why this is the case. The great French chemist and founder of microbiology, Louis Pasteur (1822-1895), "conjectured that molecular chirality in the living world is the product of some universal chiral force or influence in nature" (Barron, 2008, p. 191). Han (Department of Pharmacy, Medical College of Xiamen University) discusses the profound significance of homochirality among all living things:

> It is now recognized that all of the crucial biopolymers associated with life are homochiral (Bonner, 2000). Therefore, the source of homochirality is one of the most important topics in the research on the origin of life. In the case of these 20 protein amino acids, the origin of selection for their homochirality is still a puzzle. (Da Xiong, Hai Yan, Zhi Liang, An Fu, & Yu Fen, 2010, p. 572).

Finally, even more puzzling is the fact that when amino acids are created in the laboratory they are 50% left-handed and 50% right-handed. How then can one explain that all living things are constructed of left-handed amino acids? Miller and Urey's experiment yielded a mixture of four amino acids - 50% left-handed and 50% right-handed. Professor of Chemistry Lawrence Barron (2008) points out that, "Proteins consist of polypeptide chains made from combinations of 20 different amino acids" (Barron, 2008, p. 88). To combine 20 amino acids into proteins, all 20 amino acids need to be left-handed. Miller and Urey could not produce this result. Miller and Urey's experiment is still cited as a natural explanation for life; however, the experiment failed to produce any robust evidence of a natural explanation for life.

A more convincing experiment would have been if Miller and Urey had conducted a field study. Field studies are done in both the natural sciences and the social sciences (Webb, Campbell, Schwartz, & Lee, 2000). A good example of a field study in the natural sciences is a volcanologist monitoring volcanic activity. The volcanic activity occurs naturally, in the field. The volcanologist did not create the volcano in a laboratory! The volcanologist simply describes the volcano as best he/she can, using instrumentation and samples of the material that the volcano spews forth.

If Miller and Urey had found a place on the earth where all 20 left-handed amino acids were being created spontaneously, with no human intervention, then that would be a significant finding. To date, no one has ever claimed to go out into the field and find a place on earth where such a process is taking place. Evolutionary biologist Ernst Mayr (2001) summarized the failure of modern science to improve upon the Miller and Uray experiment:

> In spite of all the theoretical advances that have been made toward solving the problem of the origin of life, the cold fact remains that no one has so far succeeded in creating life in a laboratory. (p. 43)

Despite the dismal failure of scientists being able to create life in the laboratory, researchers continue to seek out explanations for the beginning of life. This is referred to as *abiogenesis*.

Abiogenesis

Scientists and chemists use the term *abiogenesis* to refer to the spontaneous generation of life from non-living molecules.

> Several millennia of chemical evolution had passed before the first living organisms (protobionts) appeared on earth some 3–3.5 billion years ago. Whatever the location of abiogenesis on primitive earth and/or in the interstellar medium, (ISM), pre-biotic molecules were created from simpler precursors, namely atoms and molecules. (Emeline, Otroshchenko, Ryabchuk, & Serpone, 2003, p. 204)

Emeline, Otroshchenko, Ryabchuk and Serpone are university researchers in the fields of chemistry and physics. They suggest that life appeared between 3 and 3.5 billion years ago. A transition from non-living to living molecules must have taken place, since we understand that we are living beings (and there were no living beings on earth prior to 3.5 billion years ago). Emeline, Otroshchenko, Ryabchuk, & Serpone conclude that, they have no idea of how this transition from non-life to life took place – perhaps it happened on earth or on some other planet!

This explanation for life does not tend to be particularly useful since it is simply a restatement of what we already know. We are alive, and there are things around us that are not alive. The famous mathematician philosopher, René Descartes stated it much more elegantly: *cogito ergo sum*, "I am thinking, therefore I exist." Unfortunately, both the observation of our existence and the observation that life began over 3 billion years ago on earth still falls short in explaining the *how* question. How did life first begin?

Rasmussen et al. (2004) are a group of scientists interested in creating artificial cells. To date they have not achieved success. In discussing abiogenesis they expanded on the philosophical conundrum regarding the transition from non-life to life:

All life forms are composed of molecules that are not themselves alive. But in what ways do living and nonliving matter differ? How could a primitive life form arise from a collection of nonliving molecules? . . . Although the definition of life is notoriously controversial, there is general agreement that a localized molecular assemblage should be considered alive if it continually regenerates itself, replicates itself, and is capable of evolving.

From the beginning of time, the ancients pondered the idea of life arising from non-life. C. L. Edwards (1900) observed the long tradition of myths regarding abiogenesis:

Before trying to unravel the origin of animal myths, it would be well to consider briefly the theories accounting for the origin of the animals themselves. The doctrine of spontaneous generation has been accepted in every age, including our own. From old meat, maggots are born, and from the gall, the gall-fly springs forth like armed Minerva from the head of Zeus. Anaximander, the first great teacher of abiogenesis, held that eels and other aquatic animals arise in such equivocal manner. Anaximenes, the pupil of Anaximander, gave a much more extended theory, when he taught that the sunlight streaming upon a slime, made up of earth and water, generates organisms. Aristotle also advanced the opinion that frogs, snakes, eels, and smaller organisms are automatically developed from the mud . . . (p. 34)

Geologist Donald Prothero (2007b) in his book, *Evolution: What the Fossils Say and Why it Matters*, tries to explain abiogenesis by discussing the formation of amino acids. Prothero concludes, "The initial building blocks [amino acids] are incredibly easy to produce, and it's a fair assumption that the Earth's oceans had plenty of amino acids and other simple organic molecules floating around" (p. 150).

Let's deconstruct the statement, "the initial building blocks [amino acids] are incredibly easy to produce." First, it is not incredibly easy to produce 20 left handed amino acids. We have already discussed the fact that living things contain proteins constructed from 20 amino acids, and that all amino acids in living creatures are left-handed. Prothero is wrong. This can't even be done in a laboratory, since synthetic amino acids are always half left-handed and half right-handed! Miller and Urey failed in 1953 to produce 20 left-handed amino acids in a laboratory experiment and no one else has been able to obtain the desired result today.

Second, a laboratory experiment only demonstrates that intelligence imposed on a chosen environment (by the experimenter) can yield a particular outcome. To discover evidence to support abiogenesis, a scientist needs to go into nature and observe 20 left-handed amino acids being produced spontaneously with no human intervention. This has never been observed.

Third, Prothero states, "it's a fair assumption that the Earth's oceans had plenty of amino acids." Why is this "a fair assumption"? Was anyone around over 3 billion years ago to observe and take notes on the composition of the earth's oceans at that time? We can make educated guesses, but these guesses will always elude certainty. It is a philosophical question of epistemology; how can we be certain that our assumptions of the atmosphere of the earth three billion years ago are accurate and valid? After all, an assumption is nothing more than an educated guess – it is not the equivalent of an empirical observation of a natural phenomenon.

Fourth, Prothero argues, "the Earth's oceans had plenty of amino acids and other simple organic molecules floating around." Microbiologist Behe (2007) points out that, "All proteins are chains that are constructed from a set of just twenty different kinds of small molecules called amino acids (the "building blocks" of proteins) linked together" (p. 247). Behe explains that "DNA carries the information that tells the cell how to build each and every protein it contains" (p. 247). If there was no DNA in the earth's oceans 3 billion years ago then there were no instructions to direct the amino acids to create proteins! Since DNA contains the code or the directions for assembling the amino acids into protein, how can amino acids assemble themselves without any instructions? This begs an even more puzzling question, where did the instructions contained in DNA come from?

Donald Prothero is a geologist; he is not a physicist like Francis Crick – the discoverer of DNA. Prothero overextends himself by making sweeping statements about the origin of life because he is ideologically bound to neo-Darwinian dogma, that argues that the origin of life has natural causes. Charles Darwin did not believe that life had natural causes and neither did Francis Crick!

Scientists Remain Clueless About the Origin of Life

What these scientists don't tell the public is that they have no idea how life began, or what the exact processes were that shaped the first living cells. If Francis Bacon's methods of scientific inquiry based upon the inductive method were strictly applied evolution would have to be discarded as an explanation for the origin of life. The reason is because Bacon's method (which is used today) is based upon drawing empirical evidence from a testable hypothesis. The simple fact is that no one has ever observed life arising spontaneously from non-life. Since this is the case, evolution must be discarded as an explanation for life. After 150 years of research, scientists today (like Darwin) still cannot explain how life first began. However, that does not stop devoted Darwinists from creating *a priori* assumptions out of thin air in order to justify Darwinian dogma. For example, the National Academy of Sciences (2008) gave the following explanation for the origin of life[24],

> **No one yet knows** which combination of molecules first met these conditions, but researchers have shown how this process **might** have worked by studying a molecule known as **RNA** [original emphasis]. Researchers recently discovered that **some** RNA molecules can greatly increase the rate of specific chemical reactions, including the replication of parts of other RNA molecules. **If** a molecule like RNA **could** reproduce itself (**perhaps** with the assistance of other molecules), it **could** form the basis for a very simple living organism. **If** such self-replicators were packaged within chemical vesicles or membranes, they **might have** formed "protocells" – early versions of very simple cells. Changes in these molecules **could** lead to variants that, for example, replicated more efficiently in a particular environment. In this way, natural selection **would** begin to operate, creating opportunities for protocells that had advantageous molecular innovations to increase in complexity. (p. 22)

Look at the list of ambiguous terms used in the passage above:

- *No one yet knows*
- *might*
- *if*
- *could*
- *perhaps*
- *might have*

[24] Emphasis has been added to the following quotation to highlight the extremely speculative nature of the statements that are given.

Imagine a prosecutor trying to convict a defendant of a crime, using such terms! The prosecutor could make the final closing argument: Ladies and gentlemen of the jury, you have heard the evidence of this case presented. Even though "no one yet knows" if Mr. Smith has committed the crime, I ask you to return a verdict of guilty. In fact, Mr. Smith "might" have committed the crime. Further, he "could" have been at the scene of the crime and we "could" be certain of these facts "if" someone saw Mr. Smith at the scene of the crime on the night of the incident. "Perhaps" Mr. Smith is guilty because he "might have" committed the crime.

If you were on this jury, would you find Mr. Smith guilty after such a weak and unconvincing argument? The National Academy of Sciences does not present a very convincing argument for evolution being an explanation for the formation of life.

If "no one yet knows" how life first formed on Earth, how can scientists who cling to neo-Darwinism be certain that their theory is correct? Clearly, there is a pattern of speculation here. This is perhaps the most blatant example of a lack of scientific evidence used to support a theory. As odd as it may sound, Darwin gave no evidence for the origin of species in his book *The Origin of Species*. What Darwin did demonstrate was how species changed after life was created!

One hundred and fifty years after Darwin, scientists still do not know how the first species originated, and Darwin's ideas are still not helpful to solve this puzzle. And yet, the ruse persists, that scientists have no controversy about the theory of evolution. The ruse persists that science can explain how life first formed on Earth. The narrative continues that there is a naturalistic explanation for everything and that science has all the answers. I argue that there are limits to knowledge and that on the topic of the first occurrence of life on earth, science draws a blank. No scientist has ever seen life spontaneously generate from non-living matter and no scientist has ever observed a single cell morph into a multi-cellular life form. We turn now to the puzzling problem of DNA and the genetic code.

DNA and the Chicken and the Egg Question

As the childhood riddle goes like this: Which came first, the chicken or the egg? Every child knows that eggs produce chickens. Many young children have seen chickens hatch from eggs in incubators. The incubators keep the eggs warm with lights and after the gestation period the young chicks emerge from the eggs. What a thrill it is for a young child to see life emerging from a shell that has appeared so lifeless for so many weeks!

Of course, the riddle we ask later in life – perhaps in high school is – Which came first the chicken or the egg? We all know that eggs hatch into chickens, but then where do the chickens come from that lay the eggs, if there are no eggs in the first place? The notion that eggs appear magically out of the earth is clearly absurd. And yet the notion that fully formed chicks suddenly appear without emerging from an egg is equally absurd. What does any of this have to do with evolution?

Any biologist will tell you that all living things beginning with single-celled creatures (prokaryotes) and progressing to multi-celled living things (eukaryotes) have DNA. In fact, no living thing has been observed on earth without DNA. And yet, DNA is always contained within a living cell, a prokaryote or a eukaryote. So, the question remains, which came first the DNA or the cell? DNA cannot exist without a cell that surrounds it and cells do not exist without DNA within them. We are faced with another conundrum, a variation on the old chicken or the egg riddle which continues to befuddle microbiologists to this day (Sankaran, 2012).

Can we observe DNA forming naturally in nature? The answer is no. There are suggestions that DNA came from RNA, however this still does not explain how either the RNA or the DNA ended up inside a cell! There is no theory that explains this. If we could observe either DNA or RNA popping up spontaneously in a "warm little pond" then we would have something to observe.

Can we observe cells forming without DNA? The answer is no. We do not see cells without DNA appearing in warm little ponds. We do see crystals forming, but a crystal is not a living thing – it has no DNA. In nature, many things form and even move naturally, but we do not necessarily say that things such as ice or wind are living creatures. In certain non-Western cultures natural phenomena such as fire, water, ice or wind may be given attributes of a life spirit and other metaphysical properties. However, in Western scientific circles these traditions are not recognized as evidence of life, in the same sense that bacteria or chickens are alive.

Here we have a true conundrum. The neo-Darwinists are backed into a corner. They are forced to explain the existence of DNA from a natural perspective. Crick (1981), one of the discoverers of DNA was so struck by metaphysical nature of DNA that he suggested that life did not originate on earth. Crick proposed something called directed *panspermia*, the notion that life on earth was seeded by some other planet. There is no robust evidence to support panspermia.

What we do know is that no one has ever observed a single cell forming out of non-living matter. No one has ever observed 20 left-handed amino acids being created in the laboratory or spontaneously in nature. No one has ever observed DNA forming through a natural process. All we can conclude from this lack of knowledge is that evolution offers no explanation whatsoever for the beginning of life. In the next chapter we will look at DNA itself and ask, Does evolution explain the existence of DNA?

Chapter Summary

We began this chapter by discussing what is taught in the public schools of America regarding evolution. We discovered that the National Science Teachers Association (NSTA) issued a statement to textbook publishers that censors the discussion of criticism of evolution (NSTA, 2013). We also found out the National Education Association (NEA), which is the largest public employee union in the United States has a web page called: "Understanding Evolution." The page has links to www.evolution.berkeley.edu. The Berkeley web site contains ambiguous information about evolution and the origin of life. First, there is a denial that evolution addresses the origin of life. Second, there is a contradictory statement that

"Evolutionary theory *does* encompass ideas and evidence regarding life's origins ("Misconceptions about Evolution," 2012).

Regarding public perception of evolutionary theory, it was found in a Gallup Poll (2006) that 36% of Americans believe God helped to develop human beings from less advanced forms and 47% of Americans believe that God created humans in the present form. In contrast, the poll found that only 12% of Americans believe that human beings had an origin that developed without God's help. The Gallup Poll also reveals that as a person progresses from high school to college and onto graduate school, agreement with the statement: "God created human beings in the present form," drops respectively from 58% to 25%. In other words, the more education that a person receives, the more likely they will not believe that God created human beings in the present form.

The Pew Research Center found that only 32% of the public versus 87% of the scientific community agree with the statement that "humans and other living things have evolved over time due to natural processes" (Kohut, 2009, p. 37). Reconciling the Gallup Poll data with the Pew Research Center data suggests that the reason that belief in a supernatural cause for human existence drops the longer that someone pursues higher education is simply a reflection of the teachers and professors who overwhelmingly affirm evolution – which is a natural explanation for all life on earth.

The origin of the phrase "warm little pond," where Darwin speculated life may have originated, was a letter written in 1871 to botanist Joseph D. Hooker. The letter was a private conversation between Hooker and Darwin and was not a proposal of a theory of the origin of life. Darwin did publish a letter, eight years earlier in *Athenaeum. Journal of Literature, Science, and the Fine Arts*, denying the notion that life could spontaneously be produced from inorganic material (Darwin, 1863b). Unfortunately, scholars today still persist in citing Darwin's notion of a "warm little pond" as an explanation for how life may have formed spontaneously on planet Earth, about 4 billion years ago (Follmann & Brownson, 2009). However, some university professors are beginning to acknowledge that universities need to make it clear that biological evolution does not explain the origin of life (Clough et al., 2010).

It is important to understand that Miller and Urey's experiment failed to produce the 20 amino acids that are found in protein in living cells. It is also important to recognize that when amino acids are synthesized in a laboratory, they are equally left and right-handed. This is problematic, says Francis Crick, the co-discoverer of DNA, since 100% of living things contain only left-handed amino acids (Crick, 1981, p. 43).

The term *abiogenesis* refers to the spontaneous generation of life from non-living molecules (Lal, 2008). There have been many theories about the origin of life going back to pre-history. Some modern researchers suggest that life originated on other planets, a notion called *panspermia* (Napier, 2004). In any case, life has never been observed as arising spontaneously from non-life and life has never been observed as being seeded from other planets. The chicken and the egg question remains, which came first: Was it DNA or the first living cell? The answer to this question continues to elude biologists, scientists and other researchers to this day.

V. Myth 5: Evolution Explains the Existence of DNA

*A program likewise resides in a computer chip,
but whereas that program has been shaped by an intelligent
designer, the information in DNA has been shaped by a
historical process of natural selection.*
Evolutionary biologist Douglas J. Futuyma (2009, p. 283)

Darwin proposed that the driving force behind his theory of *descent with modification* was *natural selection*. However, Darwin's theory gave no explanation for abiogenesis – the beginning of life itself. More importantly, Darwin never intended his theory to address the origin of life itself. On the topic of the beginning of life on Earth, Darwin (1876/1998) concluded: "But as we have no facts to guide us, speculation on the subject is almost useless" (p. 164).

The mystery of life became even more intriguing in 1953. In that year, three researchers, a post-doctorate research fellow James Watson, a physics graduate student Francis Crick and a biophysicist Maurice Wilkins authored an article titled, "Molecular Structure of Nucleic Acids." The article gave the first scientific evidence for the existence of DNA (Watson & Crick, 1953). In 1962, Watson, Crick and Wilkins received the Nobel Prize in Physiology or Medicine for their achievement (Chudley, 2000). The discovery of DNA in the 1950s and its recognition by the scientific community became one of the most profound biological discoveries of the 20th century.

With the discovery of DNA, by Crick, Watson and Wilkins in 1953, biology in general and microbiology in particular became revolutionized (Chudley, 2000). An understanding of DNA began to unlock many of the secrets of life itself. Most of us know that DNA is in the nucleus of every cell. But what exactly is DNA?

What is DNA?

DNA, Deoxyribonucleic acid is a biological molecule within all living things; it contains the blueprints for every living organism. Here is how the National Academy of Sciences defines DNA:

> DNA: Deoxyribonucleic acid. A biological molecule composed of subunits known as nucleotides strung together in chains. The sequences of these nucleotides contain the information that cells need in order to grow, to divide into daughter cells, and to manufacture new proteins. (National Academy of Sciences and Institute of Medicine., 2008, p. 4)

This is a stunning definition of DNA by the National Academy of Sciences. It is not a purely materialistic definition; the definition above is also a metaphysical definition. DNA contains two essential classifications. First, there are physical molecules and chemical bonds. Second, these molecules and chemical bonds form patterns which contain something metaphysical – *information*.

Any biochemist will tell you that the information in DNA contains the instructions that tell the proteins in a living thing how to form themselves, differentiate, multiply and grow. Therefore, DNA is both material and metaphysical at the same time. DNA is material because the molecules can be observed; DNA is also metaphysical, because information has no mass. Information like self-awareness, is a metaphysical concept.

Philosophy professor, Elfstrom (2009) gives a fascinating account of the understanding of DNA. In short, the only way to understand DNA is to think of it as a code and not a purely molecular or biological matter. Elfstrom, by recognizing that DNA is a code and not just a string of molecules has recognized the metaphysical aspect of the nature of DNA. Evolution and natural selection in particular have no explanation for metaphysics since Darwin's theories were strictly materialistic. It makes sense that a philosophy professor would be comfortable discussing DNA as a code, since philosophy often deals with non-material concepts such as metaphysics. Elfstrom is correct; information is just as much a code as it is a collection of molecules.

DNA, an Information Code

Here is another example of information being used as a code. Think of a password being used to gain access to a bank account on the Internet. What is a password? Passwords are information. Passwords can be coded into characters that can be typed. Password characters can be reduced to binary codes that act as electronic keys. A password can also exist in the mind of the person that created it. Many people have passwords and other significant information memorized. Most adults know their address, phone number, social security number, and a few critical passwords they use on the Internet and perhaps at work. As humans we acknowledge there is such a thing as a password and yet the thing that we call a password has no substance! It is the coding behind the information that gives passwords their meaning and utility. Humans use intelligence to code and decode passwords. Similarly, DNA is a code that contains information – the information of life itself. The question is: what was the process that created the code in the DNA?

We also have the examples of codes in the structure of languages. The words we speak and write represent ideas, concepts and information. English is based on a 26-letter orthography. In contrast, the Hawaiian language only has 12 letters, an ʻokina, which is a glottal stop sound, and a kahakō, marking long vowels. Letters are organized into words, and words into sentences, and sentences into paragraphs. Humans, who are members of a community, arbitrarily agree upon the meaning of the letters, words, and sentences. Language defines, culture, and culture defines meaning among the members of the language group. Human languages are metaphysical, because meaning is an artifact of the mind. The concepts of mind and meaning are both incorporeal. Likewise, the information contained in DNA is metaphysical and incorporeal.

DNA is a code; it is a metaphysical set of instructions. Unlike human language, DNA is far more complex that even the most complicated human writing system. If one strand of human DNA would be unraveled, it would be "125 billion miles" (Narby, 1998, p. 136), a distance greater than the distance between the earth and the sun.

Think of a cell as being a computer. The molecules are like the hardware. You can see the molecules; you can describe how they are connected to one another and you can observe how they interact with the other components of the cell. DNA is also made up of molecules; however, it contains something additional. DNA contains instructional information. When comparing a living cell to a computer, the molecules in the cell are like the hardware and the information that is in the DNA of each cell is like the software. Everyone knows that a computer would be useless without software. Likewise, living cells cannot reproduce or function without the information (software) contained within DNA. We know that humans created the software in computers. Likewise, in living cells we should be asking, how was the information in the DNA of every cell created? To simply say that evolution created the information or that the cell created the information is circular reasoning. To argue that living cells exist because of DNA and that DNA exists because it lives inside living cells is mere tautology[25].

Biologist Douglas Futuyma (2009) makes a very similar observation about DNA and computers, but then retreats to the standard neo-Darwinist rhetoric, that natural selection and evolution are the cause of everything:

A program likewise resides in a computer chip, but whereas that program has been shaped by an intelligent designer, the information in DNA has been shaped by a historical process of natural selection. Modern biology views the development,

---

[25] *Tautology* – something that is true by definition. It takes the following form: A dog is a dog.

physiology, and behavior of organisms as the results of purely mechanical processes, resulting from interactions between programmed instructions and environmental conditions or triggers. (p. 283)

Futuyma's statement above that "the information in DNA has been shaped by a historical process of natural selection" is pure sophistry. It is an unscientific statement that is intentionally constructed to deceive. DNA could not have been formed through the process of natural selection since the very first cell required DNA to live! Darwin made it clear that natural selection only works when there are other competing organisms. Neo-Darwinism is based on *population genetics*, a theory that is based on natural selection functioning within populations of living things (Okasha, 2012; Trajstman & Watterson, 1972; Watterson, 1975). DNA has no natural explanation since natural selection and population genetics do not apply to the formation of the very first living cell.

Most biologists agree that there was a time when there was no life on Earth and that "the earliest fossil life was found in strata about 3.5 billion years old (Mayr, 2001, p. 40). Since DNA exists in all known living things, it is then reasonable to propose the following research questions:

Q1: How did DNA appear in the first living cell without natural selection as a driving force?
Q2: What force was responsible for programming the information contained in the first DNA molecule?

Douglas Futuyma is wrong – the force that programmed the DNA in the first living cell could not have been natural selection, since there were no other living cells in existence. Natural selection was a non-existent force prior to the emergence of the first living cell!

This idea of DNA being an information code becomes even more disturbing (or difficult to grasp) when one considers the quantum physics cosmological model. Isaac Newton (1687/1803) caused a revolution in science regarding motion, gravity, optics and more. Albert Einstein (1879-1955) broke the Newtonian barriers with his equation $E=mc^2$. The new equation for the universe quantified a new reality; it stated that mass and energy are interchangeable! MIT trained physicist, Gerald Schroeder (2001) explains the significance of Einstein's formula: "The massless, zero-weight photon gives rise to the massive weight of the universe" (p. 154). The science of physics is not unaccustomed to theorizing and working with metaphysical concepts – namely the reality of photons, and other sub-atomic particles that have no mass. In addition, modern physicists are also intrigued by the idea of information embedded in the structure of the universe. Schroeder (2001) explains that quantum mechanics deals with the metaphysical reality of a sub-atomic world. Schroeder makes a startling claim based on quantum mechanics, "information is the actual basis from which all energy is formed and all matter constructed" (p. 153-154). If Schroeder is correct, then it is the information within the very fabric of the universe that has given rise to all matter, DNA and life itself!

Mendel, Population Genetics, and Genes

What do the discoveries of Mendel, population genetics theory and genes all have in common? Each of these topics points back to DNA. Gregor Mendel studied the results of inheritance and traits. Population genetics sought to reconcile Darwinism with Mendelian genetics in the 1930s. With the discovery of DNA by Watson and Crick in 1953, the very source of genetic information was isolated in the genes of the DNA molecule itself. But first, let's step back in time to the 1900s with Mendel's discoveries.

The Austrian monk, Gregor Mendel (1822-1884) conducted thousands of hybridization experiments in his monastery garden on the garden pea, *Pisum sativum*. The result was that Mendel produced a very robust data set from which he developed certain hereditary principles or laws, which became the foundation of the new science of genetics (Westerlund & Fairbanks, 2010). Mendel's law of segregation and law of independent assortment remained somewhat obscure, but were rediscovered in 1900, 16 years after Mendel's passing. So revolutionary to scientific discovery were

Mendel's discoveries and the new science of genetics, that Darwin's theory of natural selection became weakened.

The reconciliation between genetics and natural selection resulted from the work of three mathematicians who created mathematical models called *population genetics*. These models were created in the 1920s and 1930s (Okasha, 2012). The resulting truce, or reconciliation between genetics and natural selection became known as neo-Darwinism (Prothero, 2007a, p. 93). Today, neo-Darwinism still remains controversial and is not without its challengers and defenders (Daly, 2000; Trombulak, 2000).

The next major biological breakthrough was in 1953, when Watson and Crick discovered DNA (Watson & Crick, 1953) and were awarded a Nobel prize for their contributions to science in 1962 (Chudley, 2000). Francis Crick and other scientists believe that DNA is so remarkable that it could not have been the result of natural causes or neo-Darwinism, therefore certain scientists ascribe to the theory of panspermia. The theory of *panspermia* asserts that life on Earth was seeded from some other civilization, existing on some other planet (Crick, 1981; Lal, 2008; Napier, 2004; Wainwright, 2003; Wesson, 2010). At the core of this controversy regarding how life began and evolved, is the DNA molecule.

DNA research is a vast uncharted territory in biology. Evolutionary biochemist, Nick Lane (2009) has identified a particular part of the DNA molecule as the "DNA barcode" because, "The sequence can distinguish between closely related species such as humans and chimps and even classify new species from identical-looking ones" (p. 272). In addition to the coding found within the DNA molecule, it has also been discovered that DNA can repair itself.

DNA Repair Mechanisms

DNA has a very complex way of duplicating when cells divide. In addition, DNA has a built-in traffic cop that checks for the proper duplication of DNA when cell division occurs. If an error takes place this traffic cop takes over and corrects the error. This process is called the DNA repair mechanism (Iyama & Wilson, 2013). Understanding repair mechanisms in DNA, how they function properly and how they malfunction is leading to new pioneering cancer research. There is a known association between malfunctioning DNA repair mechanisms and the proliferation of cancer cells (Furgason & Bahassi, 2013).

It appears that all of life is contingent upon the existence of not only DNA but also repair mechanisms that maintain the integrity of DNA. Microbiologists Boiteux and Jinks-Robertson (2013) made the following startling observations after researching yeast cells:

> There has been remarkable progress in unraveling the diverse mechanisms that deal with damage to the DNA double helix and with errors introduced during DNA synthesis. Genetic studies have elucidated the high degree of redundancy built into these systems, with the net effect being the maintenance of an extraordinarily stable genome in the face of constant internal and external assaults. (p. 1050)

How did this "high degree of redundancy" get built into the system of DNA synthesis? Redundancy is a well-known concept used in critical systems. The lunar space exploration program developed by NASA had redundant systems onboard in case one system (or computer) failed. Modern airplanes have redundant systems built into them for the same reason - so that if a critical control system fails, another system will be available so that the plane can be landed safely. How do cells in general and DNA in particular, develop a repair mechanism and redundancy beginning with the very first cell on Earth?

The existence of DNA repair mechanisms within a cell is particularly problematic for evolutionary theory. How could the first cell evolve with a DNA repair mechanism since non-existence of the repair mechanism leads to cancer, and death? Both natural selection and descent with modification have no explanatory power when describing the emergence of the first living cell. It is almost as if the DNA repair mechanism "knows" what the correct sequence is, similar to how a computer virus detection program sniffs out a virus on a computer and then quarantines the infected program. In the case of virus detection programs, we all understand that a human wrote the virus detection program. In the case of living cells, these discoveries lead to an important research question: What process wrote the DNA repair mechanism code?

Molecular Design and Panspermia

Francis Crick (1916-2004), the co-discoverer of DNA was so struck with the complexity of life that he could not arrive at the same conclusion that Futuyma made, that life on earth is the result of a natural process powered by natural selection (Crick, 1981; Robertson, 2004). Crick was startled by not only the complexity of life, but also the remarkable uniformity of all life. In particular, Crick was struck by the fact that all life transforms genetic information through nucleic acids, called DNA. Crick (1981) describes DNA in the following manner:

> The nucleic acid language has just four distinct letters, there are sixty-four possible triplets (4 X 4 X 4). . . Thus, all living things use the same four-letter language to carry genetic information. All use the same twenty-letter language to construct their proteins, the machine tools of the living cell. All use the same chemical dictionary to translate from one language to the other. Such an astonishing degree of uniformity was hardly suspected as little as forty years ago, when I was an undergraduate. (p. 47)

Crick's conclusion is that the remarkable uniformity of the machine-like structure of a living cell was not the result of a natural process of evolution on earth. Crick suggested that the origin of life itself came from bacteria being shot through space on a spaceship from another civilization, from another planet. Crick (1981) calls this theory *directed panspermia*.

> Directed Panspermia – postulates that the roots of our form of life go back to another place in the universe, almost

certainly another planet; that it had reached a very advanced form there before anything much had started here; and that life here was seeded by microorganisms sent on some form of spaceship by an advanced civilization. (p. 141)

Crick is clearly a brilliant scientist and we owe the secrets of unlocking the genetic code to both Crick and Watson. But it should be noted here that Crick is also a committed materialist. His dilemma is that he understands the impossibility that life could ever evolve on earth by unguided natural causes. Crick (1981) states his dilemma, when examining the origin of life:

An honest man, armed with all the knowledge available to us now, could only state that in some sense, the origin of life appears to be almost a miracle, so many are the conditions which would have had to have been satisfied to get it going. (p. 88)

Scientists are not supposed to use the "m" word. Miracles don't occur in the naturalistic, materialistic universe. As such, Crick faces a conundrum: Where did life originate? If not on Earth, then where did it come from? Crick's thesis is therefore the following: Life came from a spaceship from some other civilization that does not live on Earth.

Biologist Stuart Kauffman agrees with Crick's thesis. Like Crick, Kauffman is also honest about the failings of natural selection to explain the spontaneous generation of life on Earth. Kauffman (2006) also puts his hope in *panspermia*:

The origin of life remains a mystery. There are several alternative approaches to the presumed origin of life on Earth, or on a nearby planet and thence transported to Earth by, say, ejecta. One approach is based on the hope of finding DNA able to replicate in the absence of a protein enzyme. This effort has failed for forty years but may yet succeed. (p. 174)

Anthropologist Dr. Jeremy Narby uses a different approach. Narby concludes that life on Earth is "minded." In other words, life was designed. Narby however, does not offer a hypothesis as to the source of the design or "mindedness" of life. Narby is open to a broader metaphysical position. Jeremy Narby (1998) points out the blind spot among the Neo-Darwinists:

> I do not intend to attack anybody's faith, but to demarcate the blind spot of the rational and fragmented gaze of contemporary biology and to explain why my hypothesis is condemned in advance to remain in that spot. To sum up: My hypothesis is based on the idea that DNA in particular and nature in general are minded. This contravenes the founding principle of molecular biology that is the current orthodoxy. (p. 145)

People like Narby who believe that nature is minded are in the minority at most university campuses. Therefore, research continues to answer the question: Where did the information in DNA come from? As a result, many scientists have turned to the stars to find an answer to this question. One approach is called SETI – which looks to the stars for answers.

SETI - Searching the Stars for Answers

The SETI program assumes that there are intelligent beings in the universe that are emitting radio frequencies that can be detected from earth. SETI stands for: "search for extraterrestrial intelligence." SETI uses radio telescopes to listen to the heavens and hopes to detect minded signals. Professor of biology Michel Morange (2008) comments:

> Despite a great deal of intensive listening (aided by four million volunteers working on their desk-top computers), no such emissions have been detected yet. This silence may mean that our means of listening are inappropriate . . . Or it may simply mean that there are no intelligent extraterrestrial

civilizations, and that the human phenomenon found on Earth is exceedingly rare, perhaps even unique in the universe. (p. 100)

What did Darwin Believe About the Origin of Life?

It has been said that in writing a book or presenting scientific paper that the beginning and the ending are the most important parts. The beginning sets up the literature, a statement of the problem and often a research question. The ending summarizes the findings and includes a discussion that interprets the data so that there is meaning and context within the scientific literature. It is within this framework that it is not a stretch to assume that the last sentence in Darwin's (1876/1998) *On the Origin of Species* was an extremely important statement:

> There is a grandeur in this view of life, with its several powers, having been originally breathed by the Creator into a few forms or into one, and that, whilst this planet has gone cycling on according to the fixed law of gravity, from so simple a beginning endless forms most beautiful and most wonderful have been, and are being evolved. (p. 649)

Darwin wrote that life was "originally breathed by the Creator." Such a statement is an anathema to any dedicated materialist or atheist. The statement appears in the last five editions of Darwin's *On The Origin of Species*. The words "by the Creator" appeared in editions 2 through 6; these three words did not appear in first edition.

I want to share a brief story. I was having a discussion with a professor of history in the teachers' work room at a university. I mentioned to him that Darwin credited the first life on earth to the Creator. He responded, "Oh yes, I knew about that. It was added in the last edition." Well, a number of years have now passed since that conversation. All of the versions of Darwin's *On the Origin of Species* can be easily looked up online with .pdf and text versions at the Darwin Online web site (http://darwin-online.org.uk). As it turns out, my professor friend had the truth reversed: The first edition omitted the phrase "by the Creator," and the five editions that followed added the three-word phrase! The conclusion is simple; Darwin was open to the idea that a Creator was responsible for the first life. In fact, Darwin was so open to the idea that he included "by the Creator" in the last 5 out of 6 editions of his book, *On the Origin of Species*. [26]

---

[26]   The last sentence in the **first edition** of *On the Origin of Species* reads, "There is grandeur in this view of life, with its several powers, having been originally breathed into a few forms or into one; and that, whilst this planet has gone cycling on according to the fixed law of gravity, from so simple a beginning endless forms most beautiful and most wonderful have been, and are being, evolved." (Darwin, 1859, p. 490)

The last sentence in the **second edition** of *On the Origin of Species* reads, "There is grandeur in this view of life, with its several powers, having been originally breathed **by the Creator** into a few forms or into one; and that, whilst this planet has gone cycling on according to the fixed law of gravity, from so simple a beginning endless forms most beautiful and most wonderful have been, and are being, evolved." (Darwin, 1860, p. 490)

The last sentence in the **third edition** of *On the Origin of Species* reads, "There is grandeur in this view of life, with its several powers, having been originally breathed **by the Creator** into a few forms or into one; and that, whilst this planet has gone cycling on according to the fixed law of gravity, from so simple a beginning endless forms most beautiful and most wonderful have been, and are being, evolved" (Darwin, 1861, p. 525)

The last sentence in the **fourth edition** of *On the Origin of Species* reads, "There is grandeur in this view of life, with its several powers, having been originally breathed **by the Creator** into a few forms or into one; and that, whilst this planet has gone cycling on according to the fixed law of gravity, from so simple a beginning endless forms most beautiful and most wonderful have been, and are being, evolved" (Darwin, 1866, p. 577)

The last sentence in the **fifth edition** of *On the Origin of Species* reads, "There is grandeur in this view of life, with its several powers, having been originally breathed **by the Creator** into a few forms or into one; and that, whilst this planet has gone cycling on according to the fixed law of gravity,

Chapter Summary

This chapter addressed the myth that evolution explains the existence of DNA. Biologist Futuyma recognizes that computer chips have coded information in them that are the result of an "intelligent designer," however, Douglas Futuyma asserts *a priori* that DNA is the result of natural selection (2009, p. 283). As it turns out, Futuyma's bold claim is not backed up by any scientific literature since: 1) no one has ever observed life springing from non-organic material and; 2) natural selection only works when there are other competing living organisms – there were no living organisms competing with each other, before the first living cell appeared on earth approximately 3.5 billion years ago!

In 1953, Watson and Crick discovered DNA: Deoxyribonucleic acid (Watson & Crick, 1953). More than 50 years after its discovery scientists still are mystified by the complexity of the DNA molecule. The great mystery of the DNA molecule is that it is both physical (made up of molecules) and metaphysical (information) in composition. The National Academy of Sciences (2008) acknowledges the metaphysical aspect of DNA in the following manner: "The sequences of these nucleotides contain the information that cells need in order to grow" (p. 4). Information is metaphysical; it exists in the realm of mind and ideas. What is most stunning is that the DNA inside of cells contains all the instructions for how proteins will form, differentiate, grow and multiply. DNA essentially is the code of life. Finally, we also learned that quantum mechanics reveals that information permeates every aspect of our universe; information is

---

from so simple a beginning endless forms most beautiful and most wonderful have been, and are being, evolved" (Darwin, 1869, p. 579)

The last sentence in the **sixth edition** of *On the Origin of Species* reads differently than the preceding five editions, "There is grandeur in this view of life, with its several powers, having been originally breathed **by the Creator** into a few forms or into one; and that, whilst this planet has gone cycling on according to the fixed law of gravity, from so simple a beginning endless forms most beautiful and most wonderful have been, and are being evolved" (Darwin, 1876, p. 429)

paradoxically an inescapable metaphysical reality. In other words, it is the reality of the existence of the information in the universe that defines the reality that we observe and interact with every day!

What we know today as the theory of evolution began as the theory of descent with modification driven by natural selection. In the 1900s Darwin's theories were in trouble. An Austrian Monk, Gregor Mendel had worked out a series of laws regarding generational inheritance, and hybridization. His findings became the bases of the science of genetics. It was not until the 1930s that three mathematicians, Fisher, Haldan and Wright worked out mathematical formulas that reconciled natural selection with genetics. The mathematical equations, assumptions, and methodology became known as *population genetics* (Okasha, 2012) from which emerged the present day dominant paradigm in biology known as *neo-Darwinism* (Prothero, 2007a).

The next major leap forward occurred in 1953 when Watson and Crick discovered DNA (Watson & Crick, 1953) and were awarded a Nobel prize for their contributions to science in 1962. Shocking to some, Francis Crick was so taken with the complexity of DNA that he did not believe it could have risen naturally on earth. Crick and other scientists today choose to believe in the theory of panspermia, the notion that life was seeded from some other civilization, on some other planet (Crick, 1981; Lal, 2008; Napier, 2004; Wainwright, 2003; Wesson, 2010). Today, molecular biologists continue to be fascinated with new discoveries regarding the working of DNA including the discovery of DNA repair mechanisms (Iyama & Wilson, 2013). Researchers have also discovered that there is a known association between malfunctioning DNA repair mechanisms and the proliferation of cancer cells (Furgason & Bahassi, 2013).

It is important to underscore the fact that Darwin's theory of descent with modification never intended to address the question of the origin of life itself. In light of this gap, it is not surprising that theories such as *panspermia* or notions that the universe is guided and "minded" (Narby, 1998) will arise to fill the gap that Darwin intentionally left wide open. Some scientists have put their belief in panspermia to the empirical test by participating in the SETI program. SETI stand for "search for extraterrestrial intelligence."

SETI radio telescopes have been searching the universe for signs of intelligent life for decades but still have discovered no evidence (Waldrop, 2011).

Darwin wrote six editions of his book *On the Origin of Species*. In editions 2 through 6, Darwin (1876/1998) concluded his book with the following statement:

> There is a grandeur in this view of life, with its several powers, having been originally breathed by the Creator into a few forms or into one, and that, whilst this planet has gone cycling on according to the fixed law of gravity, from so simple a beginning endless forms most beautiful and most wonderful have been, and are being evolved. (p. 649)

Darwin's statement speaks for itself, he clearly allows an opening for "the Creator" in the process of the origin of life – however, since Darwin adds no further explanation of his view of the role of the Creator, it is left for the reader to fill in the gap. That being said, one should take extreme caution in interpreting Darwin's inclusion of "the Creator" in the conclusion of *On the Origin of Species*, since Darwin was a self-professed agnostic (Darwin & Darwin, 1887, pp. Chapter 7 - Religion).

VI. Myth 6: Evolution Explains Multi-Celled Living Things

Most remarkably, *The Origin of Species*
said very little about, of all things,
the origins of species.
Evolutionary biologist Lynn Margulis [27]

*The origin of the eukaryotes was arguably
the most important event in the whole
history of life on Earth.*
Evolutionary biologist Ernst Mayr [28]

This chapter examines the myth that evolution explains the emergence of multicellular living things. Darwin never addressed the question of how life changed from single-celled organisms to multi-celled living things. But let's not get ahead of ourselves as Mayr points out the origin of eukaryotes was the most important event in the history of earth. In this chapter, we will be discussing both *prokaryotes* (single-celled life, such as bacteria) and eukaryotes. *Eukaryotes* can be both single-celled (also called *protists*) and multi-celled (plants, animals, and any other multi-celled life).

---

[27]   Publisher's description of *Symbiotic Planet: A New Look At Evolution* by Lynn Margulis (1998)

[28]   (Mayr, 2001, p. 47)

There are no multi-celled prokaryotes. In this chapter, we will discuss the profound differences between prokaryotes and eukaryotes and how evolutionary theory falls short in explaining their existence.

In Darwin's time, the cell was considered to be a simple organism; the complexity of a living cell had not been described yet and DNA would not be discovered until the 20th century. Most remarkably, Darwin completely omitted any discussion of single-celled life in the first edition of *On the Origin of Species* (1859). In the first edition of his book, Mr. Darwin discussed hive bees in detail and their instinctive behavior of making cells to create honeycombs. In the sixth edition of *On the Origin of Species* (1876/1998), Darwin does mention microscopic life briefly. Darwin first poses the question about how life began and then he answers his own question by supposing what the philosopher Herbert Spencer would say:

> Mr. Herbert Spencer would probably answer that, as soon as simple unicellular organisms came by growth or division to be compounded of several cells, or became attached to any supporting surface, his law "that homologous units of any order become differentiated in proportion as their relations to incident forces become different" would come into action. But as we have no facts to guide us, speculation on the subject is almost useless. (p. 164)

The term *unicellular* was defined as "consisting of a single cell" in the sixth edition of *On the Origin of Species*; the word unicellular does not appear in the first edition. Darwin described unicellular life as being "simple." In this chapter, we will see that prokaryotes are far from simple, in fact they are far more complex than anything that humans have ever created. Darwin was wrong on this assessment: Unicellular life is the antithesis of simple. But let us move the story forward about 100 years after Darwin published *On the Origin of Species*, for it was not until the 1950s that any evidence of Precambrian life was ever discovered.

Precambrian Microfossils

Darwin was also frustrated with the fact that geologists had not discovered any fossil evidence of life prior to the Cambrian period (541–490 million years ago[29]). In fact, it was not until the 1950s that any evidence of life prior to the Cambrian was discovered. Geologist Stanley Tyler and paleontologist Elso Barghoorn (1954) published a paper that pushed back the study of early life 2 billion years! They found evidence of microscopic life at "Schreiber Beach, Ontario on the north shore of Lake Superior" in a gunflint formation that overlooks the lakeshore (Dott, 2000). Today, the microscopic life that Tyler and Barghoorn discovered is classified as fossilized bacteria (cyanobacteria and iron-oxidizing bacteria). Biologist Lynn Margulis comments that Elso Barghoon Jr., (1915-1984) more than any other scientist, changed our views of Precambrian life (Margulis & Knoll, 2005).

Why did 100 years have to pass before any life was discovered prior to the Cambrian period? Perhaps scientists were looking for something too large, fossils that could be seen by the eye, instead of microfossils. Or, perhaps it was a combination of serendipity and new research techniques. The rock samples were sliced to 0.03 millimeter sections to be examined under a microscope. In addition, the samples were examined because a geologist was looking for coal and not Precambrian life at all (Margulis & Knoll, 2005)!

Today, paleobiologists and professors of earth sciences, J. William Schopf and Anatoliy B. Kudryavtsev (2010) note that microscopic fossil research has been progressing rapidly with the advancement of new research tools that allow scientists to see 3D images inside of rocks without damaging the rocks themselves. What is truly remarkable is that many of the microscopic images produced from these ancient Precambrian rocks contain microscopic fossils that are essentially identical to microscopic life today!

Bacteria were the first forms of life on earth, and bacteria have essentially not changed since they first appeared on Earth more than 3.5 billion years ago (Schopf, 1993). Cyanobacteria, are the

---

[29]   (Margulis & Knoll, 2005)

oldest known fossils on Earth. The oxygen that we breathe today is the result of *cyanobacteria*, which are capable of photosynthesis. Cyanobacteria are also referred to as "blue-green algae;" they are microscopic but are visible when they cluster in colonies.

It is important to note, that single-celled life forms ruled the Earth for about 3 billion years before multicellular eukaryotes appeared. Scientists explain that sufficient oxygen needed to be present in the atmosphere in order to support plants and animals; this took place before the Cambrian period. The French botanist Jean-Baptiste Lamarck (1744-1829), proposed a theory that life diversified as the result of time and environmental changes. Even though Lamarckism has been dismissed in favor of neo-Darwinism, Lamarck was partially correct. Without sufficient oxygen in the atmosphere, human beings and animals that breathe oxygen would not exist. Multicellular life was preceded by unicellular bacteria by about 3 billion years! The true rock stars of life on Earth are cyano-bacteria, for they have the longest enduring track record.

Five Kingdoms or Three Domains?

Before we begin to discuss the first living cells on earth, it is nec-essary to touch on the subject of *taxonomy* – the branch of science concerned with classification of living organisms. Taxonomy began with Carolus Linnaeus (1707-1778) who published *Systema Naturae* in 1735. Linnaeus began with three kingdoms: plants, animals and minerals. Since minerals are non-living substance, they are now separated from biological taxonomy. Minerals have their own clas-sification in the periodic table of elements. So, without minerals to muddle things up, it should now be simple to classify life, correct? Not exactly. Emily Case (2008) describes the classification problem in *American Biology Teacher*:

> Depending on the textbook, the teachers, and the state cur-riculum, these students learned to classify all live beings into three, or five, or six major groups, called either "kingdoms" or "domains."

The highest level of classification is *kingdom*. The five kingdoms are: 1) Prokaryotes (bacteria), 2) Eukaryotes (both multi-celled and single-celled, protists), 3) plants, 4) animals, and 5) fungi (Case, 2008; Margulis & Sagan, 2002, p. 54). Biology teacher Emily Case (2008) points out that there is a competing classification system called three *domains*, that does away with the five kingdoms entirely

The notion to create a new taxonomy called *domain* was a radical one. It was advanced by biophysicist Carl Woese (1928–2012). In 1990, Woese and colleagues wrote a paper that proposed a new taxon called *domain* that would be placed above *kingdom* (Woese, Kandler, & Wheelis, 1990). The paper was initially received with much controversy, but over the last few decades the concept has grown in acceptance. The three *domains* are referred to as: bacteria, archaea and eucarya. Today, these three domains appear in many articles and biology textbooks. Unfortunately, the only thing that is consistent about how these three domains came into existence is that there is little consensus among scholars and educators! All of this becomes a bit confusing when biologists can't seem to agree on the taxonomy of the three domains.

Then there is the question of the five kingdoms. Are the five kingdoms still the highest level of classification or have they been superseded by the three domains? To add to the confusion, professor of evolutionary biology Thomas Cavalier-Smith proposes a new six kingdom taxonomy (Cavalier-Smith, 1998). Finally, bacteria are so diverse that many taxonomists and biologists prefer to classify them at the species level and simply declare that it is impossible to identify and classify all the bacteria on Earth; such a task is analogous to counting the gains of sand on this planet. Professor of environmental engineering, Thomas P. Curtis (Curtis, Sloan, & Scannell, 2002) and colleagues used advanced mathematical computations to arrive at the following estimates of bacterial diversity on Earth:

We are also able to speculate about diversity at a larger scale, thus the entire bacterial diversity of the sea may be unlikely to exceed 2×10^6, while a ton of soil could contain 4×10^6 different taxa. (p. 10,494)

What makes this debate even more interesting is the proposal of an extinct LUCA, the noble monster in our past. Researcher at the Institute of Genetics and Biophysics, Massimo Di Giulio (2011) is continuing the research to discover the LUCA (Last Universal Common Ancestor) of the three domains. Of course, this is a difficult search since the LUCA (if it ever lived) is extinct and today, there have been no discoveries of micro-fossil evidence of the LUCA. The LUCA is therefore inferred to exist, through genomics and population genetics (Penny & Poole, 1999).

The Earliest Life - The Prokaryotes

There are divisions between bacteria, archaea and eukaryote. Some biologists would not classify bacteria and archaea as prokaryotes since archaea share some characteristics with prokaryotes. However, bacteria and archaea are both single-celled and neither organism has a nucleus. Here is a definition of *prokaryote* from the *Encyclopedia Britannica* online:

Prokaryote - Any organism that lacks a distinct nucleus and other organelles due to the absence of internal membranes. Bacteria are among the best-known prokaryotic organisms. The lack of internal membranes in prokaryotes distinguishes them from eukaryotes. ("Prokaryote," 2013)

The history of life on earth is dominated by single-celled living things. The exact date that life began is disputed among biologists. Professor of Geology and staunch defender of evolution, Donald Prothero (2007a) states that "the oldest fossils that are clearly formed by living things are microscopic fossils of cyanobacteria . . . from 3.5 billion year old rocks" (p. 145). Our best guess is that life first appeared between 3.8 and 3.5 billion years ago as bacteria.

These bacteria, or *cyanobacteria*, as Prothero describes them (found in fossilized form in Western Australia) –can be grouped in a category of life known as *prokaryotes* [proh-kar-ee-ohts]. The prokaryotes thrived on earth for approximately 1.5 billion years before the advent of the more advanced eukaryotes; the first eukaryotes were single-celled and they contained a nucleus. Prokaryotes do not contain a discrete nucleus inside of a cell. This means that the genetic material, found in DNA within prokaryotes is not inside of a nucleus (as in the cells of plants and animals). Prokaryotes are also the smallest known single unicellular life form. Evidence of prokaryotic life has been found in rocks dated 3.5 billion years old (Schopf, 1993; Schopf & Kudryavtsev, 2010).

Microbiologists have struggled to identify different categories of prokaryotes (eubacteria, archaebacteria, et al.). According to Mayr, there is still controversy among scientists on how best to categorize the different forms of prokaryotes. "How they [prokaryotes] are related to each other and how they are to be classified is still rather controversial" (Mayr, 2001, p. 44).

Let me make an important side comment here. Mayr is telling us that scientists do not agree with each other about how to classify the first form of life found on earth – the prokaryotes. Prokaryotes still exist today. No one knows how many varieties there are because no one has classified all of them. Classification of prokaryotes is far from complete and is still in the early stages with new tools for the automation and delineation of prokaryotic species being developed (Mende, Sunagawa, Zeller, & Bork, 2013). Let me repeat. Scientists do not agree with each other on how to classify the first forms of life on Earth – namely bacteria that have existed for over 3.5 billion years with virtually no change! The next time someone tells you that all scientists agree with one another on any topic – you should be skeptical. Scientists are trained to follow the evidence and disagree with each other if the evidence is not clear.

Let us leave the controversy of classification of prokaryotes; this is the type of controversy that scientists love to have slugfests over in scientific journals and conferences – theirs is a war of words. Let us continue now to another controversial topic. How did the prokaryote appear?

The Story of Prokaryotes - The Story of Life Itself

It is one thing to define and describe what a prokaryote is. It is another thing to describe how it appeared on Earth. We have already discussed the LUCA concept, the existence of a Last Universal Common Ancestor of the three domains (Penny & Poole, 1999). But this only kicks the can down the road since it begs the question: How did the LUCA get here?

Clearly, the unraveling of the story of the appearance of the prokaryote is the story of life itself on Earth. It is far from simple as Darwin surmised. Much of this topic was already discussed in Chapter IV which discussed the origin of life, so I won't cover that same territory here. What is significant is that there are some researchers that are focusing on how the first prokaryote developed.

There is evidence that life first emerged about 3.5 billion years ago (Schopf, Kudryavtsev, Agresti, Wdowiak, & Czaja, 2002; Sharma & Shukla, 2009). What is not clear is how prokaryotes were formed some 3.5 billion years ago. Some have suggested that a proton motive force is responsible for the emergence of the DNA and prokaryotes (Maier, Chen, Dubnau, & Sheetz, 2004). Evolutionary biochemist, Nick Lane (Lane, Allen, & Martin, 2010) traces the theory of a proton motive force to chemist and 1978 Nobel prize winner Peter Mitchell, who suggested a chemical/electrical force in cells that produces energy (Maloney, Kashket, & Wilson, 1974). Research continues regarding the proton motive force inside bacteria (Ollis, Manning, Held, & Postle, 2009). However, there is no clear theory of how this force may have contributed to the beginning of life itself.

One of the more popular notions today is that life may have begun in extremely harsh undersea environments, like the deep undersea volcanic vents that we observe today. This theory was advanced because life has been observed surviving under these harsh undersea conditions. Some of these conditions include anoxic (lacking oxygen) undersea environments (Danovaro et al., 2010). The theory is that the energy from the thermal vents supplied the catalyst for the beginning of life. There are a group of theories that are being floated including the pre-biotic broth theory (building blocks of life were present in the past) and the RNA world theory. In both cases, neither has been observed in nature and both theories are theoretical constructs (Martin, Baross, Kelley, & Russell, 2008; Russell, Hall, & Martin, 2010).

At present, scientists still have no idea how the first prokaryote developed. Interestingly, prokaryotes are still with us today (after 3.5 billion years) and contrary to Darwin's pronouncement as being simple, prokaryotes and the DNA code that contains the secret of life is still a mystery. Scientists understand the function of DNA, but they can be certain of neither its origins nor the source of the elusive metaphysical information that is contained within DNA. It is also a mystery that after 3.5 billion years, DNA remains remarkably stable; all living things on Earth contain DNA.

Professor Ward, a professor of Geological Sciences and Curator of Paleontology at the University of Washington in Seattle, with Donald Brownlee, Professor of Astronomy at the University of Washington in Seattle commented on the stability of the genetic code in bacteria:

> The genetic code of many microbes is still very basic – and probably not much different from that of types living over 3 billion years ago. The bacteria and archaeans appear to be highly conserved; that is, they are true living fossils. (Ward & Brownlee, 2004, p. 87)

Complexity of the Prokaryotic Cell

Microbiologists Fabienne F. V. Chevance and Kelly T. Hughes (2008) describe the motor that propels bacteria in the following manner: "The bacterial flagellum is one of the most remarkable structures in nature: a complex self-assembling nanomachine that allows bacteria to move in their environment" (p. 455). The bacterial flagellum is only one small part of the prokaryotic cell. A prokaryote may have many flagella that propel it forward in its environment. This ingenious structure has been compared to a machine, when describing its components and machine-like efficiency.

Microbiologists Chevance and Hughes are clearly baffled by the high degree of complexity that has been observed in the flagellum of bacteria, but they are committed to *materialism* – the doctrine that reality is the result of natural processes. Therefore Chevance and Hughes (2008) declare the natural causes of bacterial flagellum *a priori*[30]:

Finally, it seems that the bacterial flagellum is a structure of great complexity. In an attempt to understand why, it is not necessary to resort to intelligent designers, because surely a designer would have fashioned a simpler structure and gene regulation system. (p. 463)

Most biologists and scientists will declare that science and religion should not mix. What is fascinating with the above passage is that the authors admit the incredible complexity of the bacterial flagellum which they have discovered, but they quickly reject any sort of "intelligent designer" argument that may arise from the audience. This is an important point, because all scientific papers are written with an audience in mind – primarily other scientists.

Even more oddly, Chevance and Hughes support their claim that bacterial flagellum complexity could not have been caused by an intelligent designer because "surely a designer would have fashioned a simpler structure and gene regulation system." By making such a statement, Chevance and Hughes have opened the door to metaphysics and have allowed themselves to be criticized outside the realm of scientific inquiry. Their statement is sophistry at the highest level! For if an intelligent Designer exists, how can the creation question the Creator?

Here are some final facts about prokaryotes. They are not classified into species. They reproduce by *lateral transfer* of genes (Mayr, 2001). This means prokaryotes reproduce asexually while eukaryotes reproduce sexually. This begs the question: Since natural

---

[30] *A priori* – from "of before" are facts, data, or assumptions that need not be proved or supported by any empirical data because they are assumed to be true.

selection selects more fit organisms from an existing gene pool, how can natural selection select a cell that reproduces sexually from a group of cells that reproduce asexually? Therefore, natural selection cannot explain the emergence of eukaryotes. In fact, the boundary between the prokaryote and eukaryote is so vast, that it is as great as the boundary between non-life and life itself.

What is a Eukaryote?

Eukaryotes are found in both single-celled and multi-celled organisms. They have a nucleus, and are also much larger (500 times or greater) than prokaryotes.[31] Unicellular eukaryotes are referred to as *protists*. Examples of common protists are amoebas and plankton. Eukaryotes differ from prokaryotes in more than a dozen ways. Here are a few examples. Eukaryotes have a nucleus; prokaryotes do not. Eukaryotes reproduce sexually; prokaryotes do not. Eukaryotes organize DNA into chromosomes; prokaryotes do not.

Francis Crick (1981), the co-discoverer of DNA describes the significance of the eukaryotic cell – the cell that appeared on earth about 1 billion years after the prokaryotic cell:

> The most significant division [of life] is between organisms whose cells have a nucleus like ours, called eukaryotes, and humbler organisms which lack such a nucleus, known as prokaryotes... These could not have been studied effectively without the use of modern equipment, such as the electron microscope which allows us to visualize the components of cells in much finer detail than was ever possible before. For this reason the eukaryote-prokaryote classification is comparatively recent, dating only from about 1960. (pp. 122-123)

---

[31] Prokaryotes are typically 0.2–2.0 μm in diameter, compared to eukaryotes which are typically 10–100 μm in diameter (Tortora, Funke, & Case, 2010, p. 101).

Darwin's theory of descent with modification gives no explanation for the origin of eukaryotes. This is understandable since - as Francis Crick points out - the electron microscope was not invented until 1960. In Darwin's time, the cell was thought to be a simple organism. Scientists are currently discovering so much about the complexity of eukaryotes that some are suggesting that taxonomy should be modified to create new kingdoms (Berney, Fahrni, & Pawlowski, 2004; Pawlowski, 2013). Anyone who studies microbiology knows that the simplest cell is far more complex than the most advanced computer that has ever been constructed. In fact, the simplest cell is far more complex than the entire city of New York! Human beings designed and constructed New York; no human being has ever designed and constructed a prokaryote. But life gets even more complex with eukaryotes – the cells that exist in all multi-celled living things.

The Emergence of Eukaryotes

The significance of the emergence of the eukaryotes on earth cannot be overstated. As Mayr (2001) summarized, "The origin of the eukaryotes was arguably the most important event in the whole history of life on earth. It made the origin of all the more complex organisms, plants, fungi, and animals possible" (p. 47).

Once again, Darwin's theory falls short: it offers no insight into the origin of eukaryotes – the most important development of life on Earth! Like prokaryotes, some eukaryotes are unicellular, such as algae and amoebas. However, there is one major difference. All multi-cellular organisms contain eukaryotic cells. If there were no eukaryotes, then the human beings, plants and animals we see today, would not exist.

The invention of the electron microscope opened new frontiers of research. Like the invention of the telescope that opened up the heavens to new research and discovery by astronomers like Galileo – the electron microscope made it clear that all cells are not equal in construction and function. It was not until the 1970s that a theory was proposed to explain the development of the eukaryotes.

These new discoveries placed Darwin's theory into the "tentative" bin. Darwin had not anticipated this because the electron microscope had not been developed. Therefore, evolution and natural selection lack explanatory power in two areas. First, there is no adequate explanation for how eukaryotes developed from prokaryotes. Second, Darwin offered no explanation for how life itself began. An attempt was made to fill one of these gaps by microbiologist Lynn Margulis.

Endosymbiosis - Lynn Margulis

In the 20th century, neo-Darwinism was faced with a real problem; there was no Darwinian explanation for the development of the eukaryotic cell. A young microbiologist named Lynn Margulis had been working a new theory to explain the emergence of eukaryotes from prokaryotes during the 1960s. Her research during the 1960s was rejected by 15 academic journals; one peer reviewer for a grant application responded, "Your research is crap. Don't ever bother to apply again" ("Lynn Margulis," 2011).

Finally, Margulis published a book that presented her theory to the scientific community: *Origin of eukaryotic cells* (1970). The book advanced a theory that at some time 2.5 billion years ago two prokaryotes merged and as a result a eukaryote was created! The theory became known as *endosymbiosis* and it was flatly rejected by the scientific community when it was first presented. Over time, Neo-Darwinists became convinced of its merit as evidence of symbiants in the natural world was observed and researched. It should be noted that prior to Margulis' persistent research in the 1960s, a similar idea of endosymbiosis was presented by a Russian biologist Constantin Mereschkowsky (1855-1921) at the beginning of the 20th century (Kutschera, 2009; Sapp, Carrapiço, & Zolotonosov, 2002).

Today, the theory of endosymbiosis appears in almost every evolutionary textbook as the explanation of how the prokaryote appeared. When searching the scientific literature on the topic of endosymbiosis, terms become a bit overlapping and muddled. Biology textbooks and articles frequently use the term *endosymbiosis*

("Cells Within Cells," 2012; Prothero, 2007a). However, sometimes the term *symbiosis* is used as in Mayr's (2001) explanation of the theory: "The first eukaryote originated by a symbiosis of an archaebacterium and a eubacterium and then by a chimaera formation of the two symbionts" (p. 45). In other words, one form of bacteria (archaebacterium) merged with another form of bacteria (eubacterium), and the result was the first eukaryote cell. Lynn Margulis introduced a new term in 2002, to represent this process: *symbiogenesis*.

Biologist Lynn Margulis and her son, science writer Dorian Sagan wrote *Acquiring Genomes: A Theory of the Origins of Species* (Margulis & Sagan, 2002). Margulis and Sagan point out that Charles Darwin never did explain how species began in his book: *On the Origin of Species*. In Margulis and Sagan's (2002) book, the term *endosymbiosis* is replaced by the term *symbiogenesis*. Margulis and Sagan explain that *symbiosis* is "the living together of organisms that are different from each other" (p. 12). *Symbiogenesis* is then a "long-term stable symbiosis that leads to evolutionary change" (p. 12). What is being proposed here is that symbiogenesis is a driving force in evolutionary change, rivaling Darwin's natural selection.

To further complicate matters, there is another variation of Margulis' theory; it is called *serial endosymbiosis theory*, or SET. Botanist František Baluška (2009) pronounced, "In the past few decades, the serial endosymbiotic theory of Lynn Margulis has been confirmed" (p. 106). Margulis' theory has come a long way since she published her first article under her former married name of Sagan (1967).

Criticisms of Endosymbiosis

Even though endosymbiosis (or symbiogenesis) theory has matured to become the new dogma among Darwinists, there remains much criticism in the scientific community. For example, biologists Martin and Embley (2004) note that,

> To this day, biologists cannot agree on how often lateral gene transfer and endosymbiosis have occurred in life's history

. . . Biologists fiercely debate the relationships between eukaryotes (complex cells that have a nucleus and organelles) and prokaryotes (cells that lack both). (p. 134)

It is important here, to pause and refresh what has been discussed about the origin of life. Scientists agree that life began, somehow, about 3.5 billion years ago. Then about 1 billion years later, the first single-celled eukaryote appeared on earth. All multi-celled creatures are eukaryotes, but all eukaryotes are not multi-celled. The single-celled eukaryotes are called *protists*. Scientists continue to debate over how the structures in the first protists came to be. There is a problem particularly with the mitochondria – the energy generator in the eukaryote. Prokaryotes do not have mitochondria (but eukaryotes do). So, the question is: Where did the mitochondria in eukaryotes come from?

The existence of mitochondria in the eukaryotic cell is mandatory and without exception: Without mitochondria, the eukaryote cannot survive; it will die. So, explaining the existence of mitochondria inside the eukaryote is a conversation-stopper for micro-biologists. In a scientific article by Embley and Martin (2006), the authors recap recent discoveries in the following manner: "the evolutionary gap between prokaryotes and eukaryotes is now deeper, and the nature of the host that acquired the mitochondrion more obscure, than ever before" (p. 623). Embley and Martin continue to describe the current state of befuddlement in the quest for explaining the development of the eukaryote cell:

There are no obvious precursor structures known that would guide a gradual evolutionary inference between the prokaryotic and eukaryotic state known among prokaryotes from which such attributes could be derived, and no intermediate cell types. (p. 626)

In a blistering criticism of endosymbiosis Poole and Penny (2007) at the Institute of Molecular BioSciences in New Zealand, begin to unmask the narrative that seems to be more ideologically based. Poole and Penny argue that the theory of a merger between archaea and bacteria, resulting in a eukaryote, is not substantiated by evidence! This is in direct contrast to Mayr's statement that "the first eukaryote originated by a symbiosis of an archaebacterium and eubacterium and then by a chimaera formation of the two symbionts" (p. 45).

Poole and Penny (2007) seem to suggest that the current explanation for the origin of eukaryotes is so weak that scientists need to ask a new set of questions:

> The question is 'who' did the engulfing. Did an archaeon engulf a bacterium? Did a bacterium, bacterial consortium, or RNA cell engulf first an archaeon (which became the nucleus) and then the mitochondrial ancestor? Perhaps nuclei emerged in a virus-infected archaeon, which then engulfed mitochondria. Which, if any of these, is right? . . . Of course, missing links might exist that could bolster one of the new theories. Because it is not possible to examine every cell on the planet for evidence, proponents could always argue that their theories are not disproved. Should we take them seriously, then? No. (p. 913)

Evolutionary biochemist Nick Lane (Lane & Martin, 2010) argues that the problem with explaining the development of eukaryotes from prokaryotes is a matter of energy and coded information, particularly revealed in the increased complexity of the DNA within the eukaryotic cell. Lane explains that the amount of energy required from a prokaryote (bacteria) to form a eukaryote (cell with a nucleus) would be 200,000 times the energy level of the prokaryote:

> Put another way, a eukaryotic gene commands some 200,000 times more energy than a prokaryotic gene, or at a similar energy per gene, the eukaryote could in principle support a genome 200,000 times larger. The implications for complexity can hardly be overstated. Whereas prokaryotes frequently make a start towards eukaryotic complexity, they rarely exhibit more than one complex eukaryotic trait at a time. (p. 931)

Of course, this narrative begs the question: Where did the energy come from? Lane does not offer an explanation; however, it seems difficult to reconcile the facts that Lane has laid out for us. If it takes 200,000 times more energy to create a eukaryotic cell from a prokaryotic cell and if a prokaryotic cell rarely exhibits "more than one complex eukaryotic trait at a time" how could 200,000 eukaryotic traits appear simultaneously? Lane continues the discussion of eukaryotic complexity by observing that,

> The eukaryote common ancestor increased its genetic repertoire by some 3,000 novel gene families. The invention of new protein folds in the eukaryotes was the most intense phase of gene invention since the origin of life. (p. 932)

This is a striking statement by an evolutionary biochemist. Lane states that new protein folds in eukaryotes were "invented." Clearly, Lane is at loss to explain what he observes and is limited by language. I do not mean to imply that Lane is suggesting that eukaryotes can think, and therefore eukaryotes invented gene complexity that is 3,000 times more complex than that of prokaryotes! Once again, it begs the question: Since a stunning new development in gene complexity took place in eukaryotes, where did the complexity and coding information come from? Lane offers us no theory to address this important research question.

Let's assume that Margulis' theory is supported and that one day two prokaryotes are observed combining with each other, resulting in the creation of a eukaryote. Let's also assume that the mitochondria suddenly appear in the new eukaryote and that the DNA is now suddenly encoded to allow the new eukaryote to reproduce sexually (because the prokaryote did not reproduce sexually). Let's assume that all these things happened at the same time: new mitochondria, new DNA encoding and sexual reproduction. This leads to another important question that once again natural selection cannot answer: How can natural selection be the driving force for the development of a multi-celled eukaryote?

This is an important question because natural selection provides no explanation for multi-celled life. Natural selection supposes that life competes with life. However, in the case of protists versus multi-celled life, life would be competing with non-life. When only eukaryotes (protists) existed on Earth, a multi-celled eukaryote was non-life. It did not exist. The protist had already won the struggle for existence against the multi-celled eukaryote by default, the protist existed, and the multi-celled eukaryote did not. Therefore, natural selection offers no explanation for the multi-celled eukaryote to come to life. The leap is so profound that it is comparable to the origin of life itself. Teleology can certainly not be an explanation. The same reasoning follows for the leap from the prokaryote to the first protist (single-celled eukaryote); natural selection cannot be invoked as the cause! To summarize:

- Natural selection does not provide an explanation for the development of the single-celled prokaryote into the more advanced single-celled eukaryote (protist).
- Natural selection does not provide an explanation for the development of the single-celled eukaryote into multi-celled eukaryotes.

In summary, here are some additional questions that remain unanswered by endosymbiosis and its variant theories:

1. Symbiants have been observed in nature, however the process of endosymbiosis has never been observed in nature. Why is this so?
2. How did the mitochondria form from two prokaryotes, since prokaryotes contain no mitochondria?
3. The average eukaryote is 500 times larger than a prokaryote. Where did the energy come from to make such an astounding transformation?
4. Where did the new DNA information (in eukaryotes) come from?
5. How was the new DNA information programmed to create all the new organelles that exist in eukaryotes?

6. Why was the DNA in eukaryotes rewritten to allow eukaryotes to reproduce sexually, since prokaryotes reproduce asexually?

Three Barriers to Explaining Life

Darwin developed a theory called descent with modification that had a natural cause, natural selection. Darwin postulated that all of life that we observe today is the result of a slow process that is driven by natural selection. However, in Chapter IV we discovered that Darwin intentionally did not propose a process for the development of the first living creature. Therefore, natural selection provided no explanation for the origin of life. With the addition of the discussion of the development of eukaryotes from prokaryotes we are now faced with three barriers to explaining the existence of life on Earth.

First, we have no explanation for the first life on Earth. Yes, there are plenty of speculative theories such as panspermia, multi-universes and undersea volcanic vents. However, none of these theories has ever been supported with evidence. Life has not been found on asteroids, SETI (Search for Extraterrestrial Intelligence) has failed and life emerging from non-life has not been observed at undersea volcanic vents.

Second, there is the barrier between the prokaryotes and the protists (single-celled eukaryotes). Various microbiologists acknowledge that endosymbiosis theory has not sufficiently explained how eukaryotes developed from prokaryotes (Der Giezen, 2011; Embley & Martin, 2006; Lane & Martin, 2010; Poole & Penny, 2007). Yes, there are narratives in high school and college text books and there are also many colorful pictures that tell the story of endosymbiosis. However, scientifically speaking the problems of mitochondria, increased programming in DNA, sexual reproduction and the development of many other new organelles in the eukaryote have not been adequately explained.

Third, there is the barrier between protists (single-celled eukaryotes) and multi-cellular eukaryotes. These first single-celled eukaryotes are referred together as *protists*. The genus *amoeba* is an example of a protist. Molecular biologist Ruiz-Trillo and fellow researchers (Ruiz-Trillo et al., 2007) point out the significance of the barrier between protists and multi-cellular eukaryotes:

> The emergence of multicellular organisms from single-celled ancestors – which occurred several times, independently in different branches of the eukaryotic tree – is one of the most profound evolutionary transitions in the history of life. These events not only radically changed the course of life on Earth but also created new challenges, including the need for cooperation and communication between cells, and the division of labor among different cell types. However, the genetic changes that accompanied the several origins of multicellularity remain elusive. (p. 113)

Figure 4 graphically represents the three barriers to life that are neither explained by natural selection nor endosymbiosis.

Figure 4 Three Barriers to Life

The Timeline of Life - It's All about Bacteria

Clearly, bacteria reign on Earth. No one knows how many bacterial species exist on Earth. Estimates range from the hundreds of thousands to the tens of millions. What is clear is that bacteria are the oldest living things on earth and that they preceded the protists and the multicellular eukaryotes by about 3 billion years! Darwin was wrong about single-celled life. There is nothing simple about it. In fact, the true mystery of life is this: Why is there multicellular life at all?

To summarize, here is a map of the timeline of life on Earth.

- 3.5 billion years ago – Prokaryote microfossils discovered in Australia (Altermann & Kazmierczak, 2003; Schopf, 1999; Schopf & Kudryavtsev, 2010)
- 2.5 billion years ago – Eukaryote protist microfossils appear (B. Rasmussen, Fletcher, Brocks, & Kilburn, 2008)
- 1.5 billion years ago? – Evidence for origin of first multicellular microfossils is difficult to determine. ("Eukaryotes and the First Multicellular Life Forms," 2013; Retallack, Dunn, & Saxby, 2013)
- 541–490 million years ago million years ago – Cambrian explosion. Tremendous variety of plants and animals suddenly appear in the fossil record (Brooks, 2012; Cotner & Moore, 2011).
- Present day life, classified in 5 Kingdoms or 3 Domains. No major changes in "morphological complexity" in bacteria for four billion years (Lane & Martin, 2010)!

Chapter Summary

This chapter has focused on the development of multi-celled life or *multicellularity* – organisms that consist of more than one cell. The development of multicellularity is considered to be the most important event in the history of life on Earth (Maynard Smith & Szathmáry, 1995; Mayr, 2001, p. 47).

There is a myth that evolution explains multicellularity; nothing could be farther from the truth. Darwin's theories of descent with modification and natural selection never addressed the rise of eukaryotic cells and multicellularity. Darwin's theories bypassed what I have outlined as the three major barriers to life: 1) the origin of life – bacteria or *prokaryotes*; 2) the origin of the protists – single-celled life, *eukaryotes*; and 3) the origin of multicellularity. The origin of life began about 3.5 billion years ago. The first eukaryotes were single-celled protists, they appeared about 2.5 billion years ago and the first multicellular eukaryotes appeared about 1.5 billion years ago. Darwin's theory of life began from the Cambrian period (541–490 million years ago) and then advanced forward.

Darwin had no evidence of life prior to the Cambrian period. Therefore, it is no surprise that Darwin's theory did not address 3 billion years of life on Earth prior to the Cambrian period. It was not until geologist Stanley Tyler and paleontologist Elso Barghoorn (1954) published a paper that documented the discovery of microbial life in a gunflint formation on the north shore of Lake Superior that that pushed back the study of early life 2 billion years! What Tyler and Barghoon found was fossilized bacteria (cyanobacteria and iron-oxidizing bacteria). Professors of earth sciences, J. William Schopf and Anatoliy B. Kudryavtsev (2010) note that microscopic fossil research has been progressing rapidly with new tools that allow 3D imaging inside of rocks without cutting into the rock samples. Remarkably, scientists have documented that the early bacteria that has been discovered in rock that is as old as 3.5 billion years shows bacteria cells that look just like modern bacteria (Schopf, 1993)!

Bacteria are extremely important to the story of life on earth. Cyanobacteria are credited with creating the oxygen (2.45 and 2.32 billion years (Gyr) ago) that we breathe on Earth today (B. Rasmussen et al., 2008). The study of bacteria has progressed rapidly since the 1990s with the proposal that three new *domains* be created in the classification of life. The three *domains* are referred to as: bacteria, archaea and eucarya (Woese et al., 1990). Bacteria and archaea are the most ancient forms of life discovered as fossilized microfossils and they still exist today. Bacteria are so diverse that they are not classified at the species level; like the sands of the sea there are just too many of them to count (Curtis et al., 2002).

Prokaryotes are the earliest form of life on earth, appearing between 3.8 and 3.5 billion years ago and are thought to have thrived on Earth for at least 1 billion years before the more complex eukaryotic cells appeared. Evidence of prokaryotic life has been found in rocks dated 3.5 billion years old (Schopf, 1993; Schopf & Kudryavtsev, 2010). Some have suggested that there was a Last Universal Common Ancestor (LUCA) that existed before the pro-karyotes (Penny & Poole, 1999).

The explanation of the emergence of the first life, bacteria and archaea continues to be controversial because Darwin offered no explanation from his theories of descent with modification and natural selection. Some have suggested that a proton motive force is responsible for the emergence of the DNA and prokaryotes (Maier et al., 2004; Maloney et al., 1974; Ollis et al., 2009). It is important to note that no scientific experiment has ever been able to observe a proton motive force generating life from inorganic matter. Other theories of the origin of the prokaryote include anoxic (lacking oxygen) undersea environments (Danovaro et al., 2010; Russell et al., 2010) and the existence of the elusive LUCA in an RNA world environment (Di Giulio, 2011; Lane et al., 2010). One thing is certain. Prokaryotes still exist today (after 3.5 billion years) and DNA is remarkably stable. DNA exists in all living things on Earth. After 3.5 billion years descent with modification and natural selection have never resulted in a form of life that does not have DNA. This fact taken for granted by most biologists but is clearly remarkable. Evolution and all other natural processes cannot improve on DNA!

The prokaryotic cell is extremely complex. The bacterial flagellum in the prokaryotic cell is one example. The bacterial fla-gellum has the appearance, structure and function of a propeller that propels a prokaryotic cell in its watery environment (Chevance & Hughes, 2008). Another example of complexity in the prokaryotic cell is *lateral gene transfer* – the asexual manner in which prokary-otes reproduce themselves.

Eukaryotes appeared about 1 billion years after prokaryotes; they are also much larger (as much as 500 times) than prokaryotes

(Tortora et al., 2010, p. 101). Single-celled eukaryotes are referred to as *protists*. Eukaryotes differ from prokaryotes in over a dozen ways. Eukaryotes have a nucleus; prokaryotes do not. Eukaryotes reproduce sexually; prokaryotes do not. Eukaryotes organize DNA into chromosomes; prokaryotes do not. Eukaryotes have an energy plant called *mitochondria*; prokaryotes do not. It was the invention of the electron microscope in the 1960s that allowed scientists to study *protists* – single-celled eukaryotes, in detail.

It was not until the 1970s that a theory was put forth that began to explain the development of eukaryotes. This is because Darwin did not address microbial life; Darwin never saw microfossils. Lynn Margulis (Margulis, 1970) proposed a theory called *endosymbiosis* in which eukaryotes were the result of a merging of two bacteria "an archaebacterium and a eubacterium" (Mayr, 2001). A similar idea of endosymbiosis was presented by a Russian biologist Constantin Mereschkowsky (1855-1921) at the beginning of the 20th century (Kutschera, 2009; Sapp et al., 2002). When the theory was originally proposed it was met with opposition and even ridicule by certain scholars. Today, the theory of endosymbiosis carries multiple names including: *endosymbiosis*, *symbiosis*, *serial endosymbiosis theory* and *symbiogenesis* (Margulis & Sagan, 2002). While endosymbiosis is commonly taught in biology textbooks today, it is not without critics.

There is disagreement about lateral gene transfer in prokaryotic cells and how it relates to endosymbiosis. It is also problematic that there are "no intermediate cell types" between prokaryotes and eukaryote (Martin & Embley, 2004, p. 626). Poole and Penny (2007) argue that the theory of a merger between archaea and bacteria, resulting in a eukaryote, is not substantiated by evidence. Evolutionary biochemist Nick Lane and colleague Martin (Lane & Martin, 2010) argue that the problem with explaining development of eukaryotes from prokaryotes is a matter of energy and coded information, particularly revealed in the increased complexity of the DNA within the eukaryotic cell. Lane and Martin explain: "a eukaryotic gene commands some 200,000 times more energy than a prokaryotic gene" (p. 931). the mystery of the energy in the larger eukaryotic cells can be narrowed to once again to the mitochondria, the power centers of the larger and more complex eukaryotes (Rogers, 2013). Mark Van Der Giezen (2011) also points out that endosymbiosis does not offer adequate explanation for the mitochondria within the eukaryotic cells.

Natural selection does not provide adequate explanation for either the first eukaryotes (protists) or the multi-cellular eukaryotes. There are three barriers to life that Darwin's theories of descent with modification and natural selection do not explain.

1. There is no explanation for how life first appeared on Earth, 3.8-3.5 billion years ago.
2. While endosymbiosis tries to explain how eukaryotes developed from prokaryotes there is no empirical evidence, the evidence used to support endosymbiosis is only inferred from genomics and population genetics and not by direct scientific observation. In addition, it is not clear how mitochondria, increased the programming of additional DNA. It is also unclear how sexual reproduction in eukaryotes developed from asexual prokaryotes.
3. There is no theory for how multicellularity came about. There have been no scientific experiments that have observed a protist becoming a multi-cellular eukaryote.

VII. Myth 7: Evolution Explains Human Self-Consciousness

The recent evolution of consciousness must be viewed
as the most cataclysmic happening since the Cambrian
if only for its geologic and ecological effects.
Paleontologist Stephen Jay Gould *(1977, p. 118)*

B iologists tell us that human beings, *homo sapiens*, appeared on Earth between 150,000 – 200,000 years ago (Mayr, 2001, p. 250; National Academy of Sciences and Institute of Medicine., 2008, p. 35). These dates have been inferred from the findings of human remains and subsequent dating of those remains through a variety of dating methods. When older remains are discovered that are identifiable by scholars as being homo sapiens, then the date for the appearance of mankind on Earth is adjusted. While this is admittedly an arduous process, the dating of the emergence of human self-consciousness is clearly, far more evasive and difficult.

When did human self-consciousness first occur on Earth? The argument could be made that physical artifacts such as cave paintings demonstrate empirical evidence of self-consciousness. Not only did the early cave paintings include drawings of animals and the hunt for food, but some of the early artists did what modern artists do today; they signed their paintings. For example, in the oldest cave paintings that have been discovered, in Cantabria, Spain, in the El Castillo cave – human hand prints can clearly be seen on the cave walls.

Cave paintings have been dated as far back as 35,700 years old (Brahic, 2014, p. 10; Walter, 2015). The first pre-historic cave paintings were discovered in Altamira, in Northern Spain, in 1868. The discovery is dramatized in the theatrical film, *Finding Altamira* (Hudson, 2016). If the time line is accurate, then biologist Gould is correct in his observation that human self-consciousness is a recent development, given that life began on Earth about 3 billion to 3.5 billion years ago (Emeline et al., 2003, p. 204) and humans appeared on Earth about150,000 to 200,000 years ago (Mayr, 2001, p. 250). Per this timeline, human consciousness occurred in the blink of an eye, in terrestrial time. The purpose of this chapter is to discuss the emergence of human self-consciousness and to examine the scientific literature to see if evolutionary theory offers any explanation for human self-consciousness. I will also examine theories of consciousness and mind. I will argue that there is no consensus as to what human self-consciousness is and that modern materialistic evolutionary theory has very little, if any explanatory power to cast light upon the "recent evolution of consciousness" (Gould, 1977, p. 118).

Human self-consciousness and theories of the mind are perhaps the most profound fields of scientific study that can be investigated. The reason is because self-consciousness and mind address the most fundamental of human questions: Who are we? What makes us human? Neo-Darwinism answers these questions in a broad-based deductive logical approach, namely: Mind and self-consciousness are the natural result of evolution. For the dedicated materialist and modern student of evolutionary psychology, there can be no other conclusion (Bolhuis, Brown, Richardson, & Laland, 2011). For as evolutionary biologist Mayr states, "How did human consciousness evolve? . . . The answer is quite simple: from animal consciousness" (Mayr, 2001, p. 282). While such a proclamation for a biologist such as Mayr may seem "quite simple," philosophers are not so quick to agree with Mayr's simple conclusion.

Modern philosophers are quick to point out the shortcomings of neo-Darwinism and scientific naturalism (Nida-Rümelin, 2014; Penrose, 2015; Piechocinska, 2016). Central to this argument is the paradox that materialism does not make room for metaphysics and yet mind is universally accepted and evidenced as the reader of this text engages in metacognition. Piechocinska (2016) observes the paradox regarding our understanding of consciousness:

> Currently we are faced with the anomaly of consciousness, or awareness. One might say that there is no scientific evidence for consciousness, as we lack the ability to measure it. And yet, to us it is even more "real" that the real physical world, as it grants us access to it and we have direct experiential evidence of it. (p. 509)

Philosopher, Thomas Nagel's book: *Mind & Cosmos: Why the Materialist Neo-Darwinian Conception of Nature is Almost Certainly False* (2012), runs counter to the modern neo-Darwinian paradigm, in that it rejects the notion that Darwinism can explain the existence of the human mind. Nagel (2012) argues, "The modern materialist approach to life has conspicuously failed to explain such central mind-related features of our world as consciousness."

Berkeley philosopher, John Searle (Searle, Dennett, & Chalmers, 1997) asserts in his book, *The mystery of consciousness*, that the understanding of consciousness is, "the most important problem in the biological sciences."

Defining Human Self-*Consciousness*

Psychologists study human behavior; in contrast, biologists typically do not. The *Encyclopedia Britannica* defines *consciousness* as: "a psychological condition defined by the English philosopher John Locke as "the perception of what passes in a man's own mind"" ("consciousness," 2017). This definition is not particularly useful since it rests on the acknowledgement that mind exists, something that philosophers have debated for centuries. If the concept of "mind" is uncertain, then Locke's definition of consciousness becomes operationally weak.

Here is the more complete definition of *consciousness* from John Locke (1690) in his *An Essay Concerning Human Understanding*:

Consciousness is the perception of what passes in a man's own mind. Can another man perceive that I am conscious of anything, when I perceive it not myself? No man's knowledge here can go beyond his experience. (Locke, 1975 / 1690)

This leads to a discussion of *epistemology*. Epistemology examines competing theories of knowledge and asks such questions as: What is knowledge? What is true? Locke raises the question, "Can another man perceive that I am conscious of anything, when I perceive it not myself?" In other words, how can one human enter the mind of another human to validate that the perceptions of another are truthful, or in harmony with one another.

The French mathematician and philosopher René Descartes (1596-1650) declared "I think, therefore I am." But he did not declare - you think therefore you are. In this sense, both Descates and Lock agreed: They both concluded that certainty of the existence of mind could only be empirically verified by the observation of one's individual thoughts. Both Descartes and Locke acknowledged that men cannot perceive the conscious thoughts of other men; in the vernacular – I cannot read your mind. In philosophy, there is a term for the person who is only certain of his own thoughts and dismisses the reality of another person's thoughts, the *solipsist*. According to *The American Heritage Dictionary*, *solipsism* is: "1) The theory that the self is the only thing that can be known and verified; 2) The theory of view that the self is the only reality" (Morris, 1982, p. 1163).

Other definitions of *consciousness* include the use of the term "awareness," awareness of one's surroundings and awareness of one's own thoughts. The *American Heritage Dictionary* defines *conscious* as, "Having an awareness of one's own existence, sensations, and thoughts and of one's environment" (Morris, 1982, p. 312). This definition is perhaps a bit more palatable for some, since it avoids the term mind. Darwinian biologists tend to reject the notion of mind, preferring that the assumption be made *a priori* - that thoughts and awareness are descriptors of chemical processes that take place in the brain. Thomas Huxley is credited with the term *scientific naturalism*, a philosophical point of view which presupposes a materialistic basis for all scientific research (Haught, 2009,

p. 922). As a precursor to modern neo-Darwinism, scientific naturalism was antithetical to Natural Philosophy (Newton, 1687/1803; Schabas, 2001), the term which was supplanted by what we now call, science. Biologist Stephen Jay Gould (1977) summed up the philosophy of scientific naturalism in the following manner:

> Darwin applied a consistent philosophy of materialism to his interpretation of nature. Matter is the ground of all existence: mind, spirit, and God as well, are just words that express the wondrous results of neuronal complexity. (p. 13)

Unfortunately, Gould's summation of scientific naturalism as it applies to mind is quite disappointing, for it avoids the question: What is Mind? Gould dodges the hard issue of mind and consciousness, by suggesting that mind is illusory.

In summary, we are faced with various definitions of *consciousness*, some which clearly choose to use the term *mind* and others that adroitly skate around the *mind*, perhaps to avoid the centuries old Cartesian mind-body dualism kerfuffle. We are even faced with biologists such as Gould who on the one hand admit that consciousness is a recent cataclysmic event, while at the same time seem to dismiss the notion that mind even exists! Whatever the motivation for various definitions of *consciousness*, we shall press on to seek a better understanding of *mind*.

When did Human Self-Consciousness Develop?

The answer to this question is generally outside of the realm of biology, because it cannot be observed directly. For example, bones and fossils offer physical evidence that can be analyzed and categorized. Consciousness, on the other hand is metaphysical. It is not the same as a bone or a fossil; it has no weight or physical properties. Of course, one could argue that consciousness exists within the brain and that the presence of a brain such as is found in *homo sapiens* is unique among living things. Therefore, consciousness is the result of the evolutionary development of the human brain.

Evolutionary biologist Mayr (2001) comments on the evolution of human consciousness:

> How did human consciousness evolve? This is a question that psychologists love to ask. The answer is actually quite simple: from animal consciousness! . . . It is quite certain that human consciousness did not arise full-fledged with the human species, but is only the most highly evolved end point of a long evolutionary history. (p. 282)

While Mayr does attempt to discuss human consciousness, he clearly fumbles the ball and shows his hand. He remarks that "this is a question that psychologists love to ask." His statement is peculiar in that he seems to insinuate that since psychologists are asking the question, that the question is somehow invalid or unimportant. Academics often dismiss (or poke fun at) other academics, that are outside of their particular field of research.

Mayr (2001) goes on to state emphatically: "The answer is actually quite simple: from animal consciousness!" (p. 282). What Mayr asserts as "quite simple" is not quite simple at all. He offers no evidence for his claim that human consciousness comes from animal consciousness. Mayr simply dismisses a profound academic question: How did human consciousness evolve? By doing this, Mayr employs unscientific deductive reasoning. I say deductive, because Mayr offers a broad-brushed sweeping generalization as evidence to dismiss the question: How did human consciousness evolve? Mayr's approach fails the *a priori* test, since it is a methodology that reaches a conclusion without any sound empirical data.

Finally, Mayr (2001) concludes that human consciousness is a "highly evolved end point of a long evolutionary history." While Mayr's statement seems to open up the door to *teleology* (the philosophy that life is not random but has an end-goal), I will choose not to pursue this criticism. I would rather comment on his assertion that human consciousness is the result of "a long evolutionary history." Indeed, it is not, according to the time-line that evolutionary biologists have given us.

- Life on Earth began about 3 billion to 3.5 billion years ago.
- *Homo sapiens* appeared on Earth about about150,000 to 200,000 years ago.
- Human consciousness emerged less than 40,000 years ago (as evidenced by cave art).

Clearly evolutionary biologists do not agree on the significance of when human consciousness occurred. Evolutionary biologist Stephen Jay Gould (1977) writes: "The recent evolution of consciousness must be viewed as the most cataclysmic happening since the Cambrian" (p. 118). In contrast, Mayr acknowledges that human consciousness is neither recent (in evolutionary terms) nor remarkable. Gould is correct: human consciousness is clearly a recent development on Earth, profoundly remarkable and worthy of exploration.

What are sound criteria to use for the advent of human self-consciousness? The following diagram in Figure 5 addresses this question.

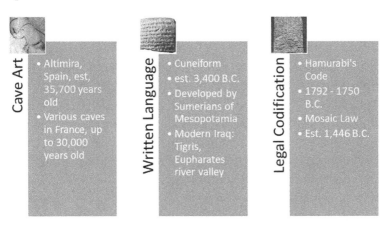

Figure 5 Advent of Human Consciousness

Returning to John Locke's definition of *consciousness* that, "Consciousness is the perception of what passes in a man's own mind." (Locke, 1975 / 1690). The chart above presents evidence of three artifacts of consciousness, evidence of what passes in a human mind.

First, there is ancient cave-art. One could argue that pre-historic cave art represents the images that passed in the mind of ancient humans that created these magnificent paintings on the walls of ancient caves in Spain and France (Hudson, 2016; Valladas et al., 2001). As is commonly said, "art imitates life." Apparently, such has been the case from ancient times until the modern age. Pre-historic humans recorded the animals that were close to them, perhaps to brag about the last hunt, or to teach and record information for a future generation of hunters.

Second, there is written language. Research regarding written language, overlaps with the field of *semiotics*, "the study of signs and symbols as elements of communicative behavior" ("semiotics," n.d.). Semiotics includes more than just written language: It includes ancient petroglyphs, which can be found all over the world. University of Colorado paleoclimatologist Larry Benson researched petroglyphs in Winnemucca Lake, Nevada and has concluded they are 10-15,000 years old (Powell, 2014). Petroglyphs are symbols, usually carved into rock; they predate Sumerian cuneiform by more than 10,000 years.

Sumerian cuneiform has been accepted as the oldest system of writing, dating back to the 4th millennium B.C. (Puhvel, 2017). Sumerian cuneiform tablets and steles (upright stones bearing inscriptions) have been found in modern day Iraq. Cuneiform writing was found in abundance in the ancient city of Ur, a part of ancient Mesopotamia in modern Iraq. Written language is a tangible artifact that supports the notion of human self-consciousness. In addition, written language supports the thesis of metacognition, evidence that humans were thinking about thinking. In other words, when one reads the written thoughts of another person, the reader is engaging in discovering the thoughts of someone other than themselves.

Metacognition has its highest form of expression in the accumulated history of knowledge. Human beings are unique in that they understood the power of written language. By creating written language, humans can accumulate and accelerate knowledge from generation to generation. Humans also have an insatiable desire to research and record history. While this was often done by illiterate societies in the form of poems and chants, societies that possessed written language held scribes in high esteem, for their ability to record the achievements of the rulers they served. This is evident throughout the world from the inscriptions on the Egyptian pyramids to the ancient Mayan temple writing in Central America; ancient rulers desired to use the written word to perpetuate their kingdoms into the annals of human history. The formation of libraries and schools of learning throughout the ancient world is further evidence of metacognition. The world's oldest know library is the Library of King Ashurbanipal, built in the 7th-century BC. *The Epic of Gilgamesh* (George, 2003) was discovered at the Library of Ashurbanipal. The library is in the ancient Assyrian city of Nineveh, located in Mosul, present-day Iraq.

Finally, legal codification is the third and highest order of evidence to support the notion of human self-consciousness. Hammurabi's Code (1792 – 1750 B.C.) is more than a writing system: It is a moral prescriptive codification of intended behavior for society ("Hammurabi," 2017). Hammurabi was a Babylonian king who brought order to one of the very first human civilizations. A moral code, or codification of laws, such as that written by Hammurabi or Moses[32], represents more than just written language. Codified laws are prescriptive in that they include a moral prescriptive directive: they tell the reader, "This is what you should do." When comparing cave art, cuneiform writing and legal codification (Hammurabi and Moses), legal codes are the highest form of evidence of human self-consciousness. A legal system of laws states the intent of the writer and gives direction to the members of society that this is the prescribed behavior. In addition, adherence or disobedience to such codified laws usually bears penalties for disobedience. Today, in modern courts of law, defendants are judged by the law if they are considered to be "of sound mind." Therefore, human self-consciousness today is not only a description of a functioning member of society but is also a prerequisite to being judged in a court of law as being mentally competent to understand and conform to the laws of a society.

---

[32]   Moses wrote the first five books of the Hebrew Bible. The fifth book, Deuteronomy, has codified laws.

Darwin's View of Human Self-Consciousness

Charles Darwin concluded that self-consciousness is not unique to mankind, in his work, *The Descent of Man* (Darwin, 1871/2004):

> If it could be proved that certain high mental powers, such as the formation of general concepts, self-consciousness, etc., were absolutely peculiar to man, which seems extremely doubtful, it is not improbable that these qualities are merely the incidental results of other highly advanced intellectual faculties; and these again mainly the results of the continued use of a perfect language. At what age does the new-born infant possess the power of abstraction, or become self-conscious, and reflect on its own existence? (p. 104)

Let us deconstruct what Darwin is saying in this passage. First, Darwin dismisses the notion that self-consciousness and higher order thinking is peculiar to mankind. He gives no evidence that other creatures possess the same capacity for abstract thought, language, meta-cognition, reason and logic that humans possess. He simply dismisses the notion that human self-consciousness is unique among living things as being "extremely doubtful." Any scientist that summarily dismisses a clear body of evidence, is displaying his or her bias. Darwin did not want to conclude that mankind was in a special category of possessing self-awareness, because this would weaken his theory of descent with modification. Darwin also asserted an *a priori* conclusion: namely, that human beings are not unique among living creatures.

Second, Darwin suggests that human self-consciousness is merely the result of the possession of "highly advanced intellectual faculties" which lead to the use of "a perfect language." This is an observation with which most scholars agree: The human capacity for language, thinking and reason is clearly highly developed. As far as we know, human beings have not been able to converse with animals about topics such as: the stock market, investment portfolios, the Super Bowl, marriage, politics or news articles. The evidence seems rather clear: Humans are unique in their ability to be self-conscious and to express their ideas to other human beings. Human beings possess *metacognition*, the ability to think about thinking.

Certain biologists do observe that animals communicate with each other, such as the "bee dance," the whale song, giant apes giving gestures and grunting and wolves howling to signal to the pack. However, these are recognizably a form of lower order communication. What we do not see among bees, whales, wolves and other animals is demonstration of metacognition. Meta cognition is higher order thinking, the ability to think about your thinking, or think about the thinking of others. For example, when we read an editorial article in a newspaper, we are reading someone's opinion of a subject. We usually agree or disagree, or perhaps partially agree and disagree with certain points of the article. This is one example of meta-cognition. Humans have never engaged in conversations with animals about nuclear physics, black holes, calculating the trajectory to the moon or the criteria for judging the best chili recipe in the United States.

Third, Darwin poses a powerful research question: "At what age does the new-born infant possess the power of abstraction, or become self-conscious, and reflect on its own existence?" This leads us into the modern field of developmental psychology and pioneering work of Jean Piaget and others (Ferrari, Pinard, & Runions, 2001).

Disagreements with Darwin's View of Self-Consciousness

There are many who disagree with Darwin's notions of human self-consciousness. One resounding area of scientific inquiry that seems to often contrast with Darwin, is the area of developmental psychology. Psychologist Philippe Rochat (2003) suggests that there are five stages of increasing human self-consciousness or self-awareness from birth to 4-5 years of age. The famous French developmental psychologist Jean Piaget (Flavell, 1996) proposed a theory of cognitive development, in which children learn through 4 stages of cognitive development and growth along with learning theory. Piaget described *assimilated learning*, which we see in structured educational systems and *accommodative learning* – which is more task oriented and experiential (Blatner, 2004; Wadsworth, 2004). Psychologist John Flavell (1996) comments that, "Piaget's greatest contribution was to be found in the field of cognitive development" (p. 200). Flavell further observes:

> Piaget helped us to accept the idea that children's cognitive behavior is intrinsically rather than extrinsically motivated. Although social and other reinforcements may influence children's curiosity and cognitive explorations to some degree, basically children think and learn because they are built that way. (p. 200)

This is a rather remarkable observation, that children are "intrinsically rather than extrinsically motivated." It seems to run in stark contradiction to Darwin's *a priori* argument that human self-consciousness is not "peculiar to man." Indeed, Piaget argues against the philosopher John Locke, who advanced the notion that the human mind is a *tabula rasa*, an erased tablet (Locke, 1975 / 1690). Flavell summarizes the opposite, that Piaget advanced the notion that "children think and learn because they are built that way."

Psychologists refer to these opposing viewpoints of cognitive development as: nature versus nurture. Piaget argued for the influence of *nature* - an inherited ability to think and learn, something built into children at birth. In contrast, the philosopher John Locke argued for *nurture*: He believed humans are born with no pre-programmed information – *tabula rasa*.

Another scientist who disagreed with Darwin's notion of human self-consciousness was Alfred Russel Wallace, the famous co-author of "On the tendency of species to form varieties; and on the perpetuation of varieties and species by natural means of selection" (Darwin & Wallace, 1858). This was the paper presented to the Linnean Society of London, which predated Darwin's famous *On the Origin of Species* (Darwin, 1860), by two years. Wallace was not convinced that the human mind is the result of an entirely natural process. Two years before the presentation of the paper to the Linnean Society of London with Darwin, Alfred Wallace (1895) published the following arguments and observations about the human brain and consciousness:

> Those faculties which enable us to transcend time and space, and to realize the wonderful conceptions of mathematics and philosophy, or which give us an intense yearning for abstract truth . . . are evidently essential to the perfect development of man as a spiritual being, but are utterly inconceivable as having been produced through the action of a law which looks only, and can look only, to the immediate material welfare of the individual or race. The inference I would draw from this class of phenomena is, that a superior intelligence has guided the development of man in a definite direction, and for a special purpose . . . We know, however that this has been done; and we must therefore admit the possibility that, if we are not the highest intelligences in the universe, some higher intelligence may have directed the process by which the human race was developed, by means of more subtle agencies than we are acquainted with. (p. 204)

Wallace's comments are perhaps quite disturbing for contemporary evolutionary biologists. Wallace, who proposed descent with modification along with Charles Darwin is suggesting that human consciousness is unique and the result of "intelligences in the universe." Clearly, this heretical notion would be rejected in an introduction to biology course in any public university today! While Darwin advanced a purely materialistic viewpoint of his Descent with Modification theory (now known as Evolution), Alfred Russel Wallace advanced a teleological theory of evolution which included the possible outside influence of a "higher intelligence" in the universe (Jones, 2015).

Speculation is not the realm of the evolutionary biologist. That is why the science of mind, if there is any such thing, is left to the realm of philosophers to opine about. While Francis Crick along with Watson cracked the DNA code (Watson, 1968), Crick in his later years was fascinated and ultimately stone-walled in his search for a scientific explanation of both mind and soul. In his book:

Astonishing Hypothesis: The Scientific Search for the Soul (1994), Crick the scientist comes full circle in his desire to close the Cartesian gap between the mind and body. Whether he accomplished his goal or not, Crick the scientist and materialist, put down one set of tools and embarked on the metaphysical journey of the philosopher, to try and explain the existence of human self-consciousness and mind. Crick (1981) is known for rejecting neo-Darwinism; he concluded from his research that DNA is essentially metaphysical (as it is information) and that it is so complex that it could not originate on earth!

Philosopher Thomas Nagel (1974) in his famous article "What Is It Like to Be a Bat?, challenged the notion of evolution and scientific naturalism explaining the existence of mind. In this brilliant and often cited article, Nagel builds his case in the following steps:

1) HUMAN CONSCIOUSNESS IS UNIVERSALLY ACKNOWLEDGED: The mind-body problem is a scientific conundrum, since human beings acknowledge the existence of human consciousness,

2) HUMAN CONSCIOUSNESS DEFIES DEFINITION: "Most reductionist theories do not even try to explain it (consciousness)" (p. 436).

3) CONSCIOUSNESS IS THE EVIDENCE OF MATERIALSIM: Since materialism postulates that all phenomena are the result of naturally occurring cause and effect mechanisms, it follows that consciousness must also be the result of materialism. But how can consciousness be the result or evidence for materialism when consciousness is not defined in the first place? Figure 6 displays classic circular reasoning, stating that consciousness is the result of materialism and the evidence of materialism is the existence of consciousness.

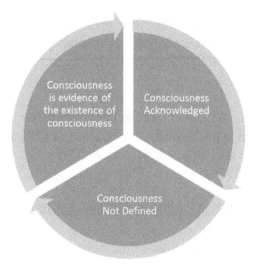

Figure 6 Classic Circular Reasoning

Nagel (1974) summarized the problem of *consciousness* in the following manner:

> It is useless to base the defense of materialism on any analysis of mental phenomena that fails to deal explicitly with their subjective character. For there is no reason to suppose that a reduction which seems plausible when no attempt is made to account for consciousness can be extended to include consciousness. (p. 437)

Just as we cannot know what it is to be a bat, we also cannot know what it is to be self-conscious as another human being. In short, we can only know with any degree of certainty our own thoughts, but we can never know with any degree of certainty the thoughts of others. As such, we arrive at the solipsist point of view: the person who adopts the philosophy that the only knowable reality is the one that he or she is aware of individually. Put another way, Nagel states:

> If physicalism is to be defended, the phenomenological features must themselves be given a physical account. But when we examine their subjective character, it seems that

167

such a result is impossible. The reason is that every subjective phenomenon is essentially connected with a single point of view, and it seems inevitable that an objective, physical theory will abandon that point of view. (p. 437)

Modern scholars continue to acknowledge that the existence of consciousness is a problem for materialists in particular and reductionism in general (Terrace & Metcalfe, 2005).

Can Evolution Explain Human Self-Consciousness?

Philosopher David Chalmers (2002) summarized the problem of consciousness in this manner:

There is nothing we know about more directly than consciousness, but it is extraordinarily hard to reconcile it with everything else we know. Why does it exist? What does it do? How could it possibly arise from neural processes in the brain? These questions are among the most intriguing in all of science. (p. 90)

While Chalmers writes candidly about the problem of consciousness, another philosopher, Daniel Dennett proposed that he tackled the problem of the mind and triumphed in his book: *Consciousness Explained* (1991). Dennett, of course rejects Cartesian mind/body dualism, in favor of his "heterophenomenological" method, a unique form of phenomenology that uses dissected mind observations as data. In any case, Dennett's approach is not without criticism.

Philosopher Abraham Olivier (2010) notes, "My contention is that while Dennett's third-person approach to consciousness is valid on an epistemic level, it fails ontologically" (p. 104). By this, Oliver was acknowledging that Dennett's heterophenomenological method has validity in its ability to gather objective data, from third-party sources. However, Olivier criticizes the causal connection between data gathered and the world in which we exist. In other words, brain waves can be measured, and external characteristics observed. The more difficult problem of consciousness was not being tackled from the point of view of the subject's consciousness. Put another way, I can ask you about what is going on in your mind and I can record responses. However, I cannot enter into your mind and record and observe the same phenomena. The mind therefore, whatever it is, is singularly observable.

David Hume (1711-1776) wrestled with the problem of the mind in his discussion of color (Hume, 1748, 1955). Hume argues that one can reason to a color, even if he or she has never seen the actual shade of color. For most people, such a notion may seem to be set somewhere between the trivial and absurd. But for philosophers such as Hume, the debate continues to this day. Are colors created in the mind, or does the mind observe colors through the eyes and then categorize variations and shades of colors from a composite database?

Philosopher Daniel Dennett published *Consciousness Explained* (1991) and then more recently; *Kinds of minds: toward an understanding of consciousness* (1996). Dennett again wrestles with the same question that Hume did: Is it possible for anyone to know with certainty what goes on in the mind of another human being? While Dennett is a master at describing evolution as a progression from simple stimulus-response to the environment, eventually to the recognition of the need of a science of mind, to understand human thinking and metacognition, the fact remains: human consciousness remains metaphysical and evolution is woefully inadequate as an explanatory vehicle.

We cannot observe the development or the evolution of the human mind as a step-by-step Darwinian process. There are no fossils of "mind." There is no physical evidence of mind. The best evidence of pre-historic mind that we have are ancient cave drawings, and yet we do not have phenomenological evidence. We do not know why early man drew the pictures on cave walls and we do not know what they were thinking when they drew the pictures. Were they bragging about their hunting exploits? Were the drawings pre-historic textbooks to teach a future generation of hunters? All we can do is speculate.

We now turn our discussion to the mind. Most doctors, psychiatrists and psychologists will agree that there is a relationship between human self-consciousness and the mind. For some the two terms are interchangeable. For others, human self-consciousness is something that humans grow into as they mature and the ability of the human to become self-aware is somehow made possible through our DNA and the capacity of the human brain. Further, research has shown that personality can be affected by trauma to the brain (Black & Black, 1982; Woodward, Bisbee, & Bennett, 1984)

Defining *Mind*

Webster's (1828/1983) *American Dictionary of the English Language* gives several definitions for *mind*:

1) Intention, purpose, design; 2) Inclination, will, desire; 3) Opinion; 4) Memory; 5) The intellectual or intelligent power in man; the understanding; the power that conceives, judges or reasons – So we speak of a sound *mind*, a disordered *mind*, a weak *mind*, a strong *mind*, regarding the *active* powers of the understanding;

The definition of *mind* from *The American Heritage Dictionary* is more materialistic, in that its authors choose to locate the mind in the brain: "The human consciousness that originates in the brain and is manifested esp. in thought, perceptions, feeling, will. Memory, or imagination" (Morris, 1982).

Dictionary.com gives several definitions of *mind*, choosing not to originate mind in the brain ("mind," n.d.):

1. (in a human or other conscious being) the element, part, substance, or process that reasons, thinks, feels, wills, perceives, judges, etc.: the processes of the human mind.
2. Psychology. The totality of conscious and unconscious mental processes and activities.
3. Intellect or understanding, as distinguished from the faculties of feeling and willing; intelligence.

4. a particular instance of the intellect or intelligence, as in a person.
5. a person considered with reference to intellectual power.
6. the greatest minds of the twentieth century.
7. intellectual power or ability.
8. reason, sanity, or sound mental condition.
9. to lose one's mind.

Clearly, *mind* is not easy concept to define. The problem is that we all refer to it, discuss it, give one another "a piece of our mind," and yet it eludes direct observation. We know where the brain is located, but where can we locate the images of a movie we saw last week, the taste of a filet mignon, inductive reasoning, deductive reasoning, or an emotional sensation? Mind is perhaps one of the most common of nouns and yet philosophers have opined about its substance and meaning for millennia.

The Ancient Understanding of *Mind*

From the beginning of recorded history, ancient philosophers and medical professionals were interested in the human mind and particularly the brain. The Edwin Smith Papyrus is the world's oldest written documentation of the human brain. It dates to 1,500 BC, but it may be a copy of a much older work that preceded it, by 1,000 years. The papyrus contains descriptions of 48 individuals with wounds to the head and brain, along with detailed medical observations. The Egyptians however, did not view the brain to be the epicenter of human intellect and consciousness. Instead they preferred the heart as the center of the cognitive self. This was reflected in the practice of mummification; the heart was "pickled in a special canopic jar, the brain was scooped out with a metal hook and unceremoniously thrown away (Mosley & Lynch, 2010, p. 232). In addition, ancient Sumerian records have revealed descriptions of the hallucinogenic poppy, and its effect on the human brain (Langone et al., 2006, p. 360).

The famous Greek physician Hippocrates (460-377 BC) argued that epilepsy was a disease that originated in the brain. The Greek philosopher Plato (428-347 BC) was not an empiricist; he preferred reason over direct observation and empirical evidence, to support his theories. Plato suggested that humans have various centers of emotion and cognition. He suggested that thinking was centered in the head, lustful desires were in the liver and emotions were centered in the heart. (Mosley & Lynch, 2010, p. 234). Even today, we talk about the heart as the center of emotion and feelings. We say things like, "I love you with all my heart" to someone to whom we are emotionally committed.

The Greek philosopher, Aristotle (384-322 BC) elevated the heart to the center of human cognition and rationality. Like the ancient Egyptians, Aristotle saw little purpose for the brain, in terms of thinking or rationality.

The debate about the center of cognition and the seat of rationality and emotions did not advance much until then Roman Empire performed human dissections in Alexandria, Egypt. This was during the period of Alexander the Great (356-323 BC). "Herophilus of Chalcedon a Turkish Greek living in Alexandria, performed hundreds of human dissections and in doing so made the first detailed examinations of our brains" (Lynch, 2005, p. 236). It is said that he not only performed dissections on corpses, but also barbaric vivisections on condemned criminals presented by the King of Egypt. During the European Middle Ages (350 to about 1450 BC), dissections and descriptions of the brain continued.

Modern Theories of *Mind* and Human *Consciousness*

Many ask the following question: What is human consciousness? Perhaps more fundamental is this question: What is the mind? The French mathematician and philosopher René Descartes (1596-1650) pioneered a theory of the mind which is referred to as mind/body dualism. Descartes began his theory by asserting an indubitable truth, *cogito ergo sum*, translated from the Latin as: "I think, therefore I am." By stating this truth, Descartes was saying that it is my ability to think (my consciousness or self-awareness) that defines my existence. From this initial postulate, Descartes reasoned to the existence of God. In addition, Descartes reasoned that the mind and the body are not identical but that they are inextricably linked to one another until the time of death. Through dualism, Descartes postulated that the mind and the body are separate entities. In other words, Descartes was conscious that he was thinking. Therefore, he intuited that conscious consciousness, as evidenced by thought was empirical proof that he existed. This is quite fascinating. Descartes reasoned that the proof of his corporeal existence was his metaphysical, incorporeal thought process!

Cleary, Descartes' theory of mind-body dualism leads to the topic of metaphysics. *Metaphysics* deals with incorporeal substances, belief systems, religion, and the realm of the supernatural. As humans, we are familiar with the term *mind*. At times, it is used interchangeably with the word "soul," in reference to our will and our emotions. While psychologists may be loath to say that they study the "soul," the field of psychology clearly centers on the study of human behavior, which is linked to the mind. The mind, our thinking and reasoning cannot be detached from our actions. Only in a court room can actions and will be temporarily separated and that occurs only when a person is pronounced legally insane or in such a state of dementia that the mind in no longer in control of behavior.

Descartes took it one step further, by developing a philosophy of mind-body dualism. He proposed a connection between the metaphysical and physical as being in the penal gland, next to the human brain. Over the centuries philosophers have reacted to, criticized and offered up competing theories of the human mind and consciousness. But the fact is the starting point of the modern philosophy of the mind was the 15th century mathematician and philosopher, René Descartes.

The mind-body dualism argument continues today and is referenced in modern scholarly papers. Arbib (2014) of the Computer Science Department and USC Brain Project, University of Southern California observed the following:

> The reader may consult Arbib & Hesse (1986) for an articulation of the philosophical debate between those who, in line with the above argument, see the "self" as embodied within

the neural circuitry and the body which contains it, and those dualists who view the self as in some sense separable from brain and body.

Some competing categories of theories of mind include:

- *Dualism* – A theory of the mind advanced by the French philosopher René Descartes (1596-1650). Descartes argued that the mind and body are two distinct entities, connected by the pituitary gland in the brain. The body is material and the mind has no physical substance. The conclusion that the mind and the body were separate was not without prior observation. For millennia, soldiers on battlefields were observed with brain injuries that rendered the body still functioning, but the mind lost to the world. Even today we use the expression; He (or she) is out of his mind. Dualism has over the centuries grown out of favor, since it is difficult to support empirically. Indeed, Descartes used biblical reasoning to advance his theory of mind in his writings, a methodology that is unacceptable among modern secular scholars. What follows are some other modern theories of mind.

- *Functionalism – The Stanford Encyclopedia of Philosophy* states:

   Functionalism in the philosophy of mind is the doctrine that what makes something a mental state of a particular type does not depend on its internal constitution, but rather on the way it functions, or the role it plays, in the system of which it is a part. This doctrine is rooted in Aristotle's conception of the soul, and has antecedents in Hobbes's conception of the mind as a "calculating machine." (Levin, 2016)

- *Parallelism* – A theory of the mind advanced by Gottfried Wilhelm von Leibniz's (1646-1716). Leibniz rejected Descartes' dualism, but also rejected a purely materialistic interpretation of the mind. To this day, scholars argue about what exactly Leibniz proposed, a sort of parallel interaction between mind and body, but one in which there was not a clear causal connection between a metaphysical entity and a physical body. *The Stanford Encyclopedia of Philosophy* states the following about Leibniz's theory of the mind:

> In a more popular view, Leibniz's place in the history of the philosophy of mind is best secured by his pre-established harmony, that is, roughly, by the thesis that there is no mind-body interaction strictly speaking, but only a non-causal relationship of harmony, parallelism, or correspondence between mind and body. (Kulstad & Carlin, 2013)

- *Epiphenominalism* has been attributed to Thomas Huxley (1825-1895), a term that Huxley did not use, but was later coined by the philosopher and psychologist, William James (1842-1910). The *Stanford Encyclopedia of Philosophy* defines *epiphenomenalism* as,

> . . . the view that mental events are caused by physical events in the brain, but have no effects upon any physical events. Behavior is caused by muscles that contract upon receiving neural impulses, and neural impulses are generated by input from other neurons or from sense organs. On the epiphenomenalist view, mental events play no causal role in this process. (Robinson, 2015)

- *Free Will* - Jonathan Edwards, president of Princeton University (1758) was the author of *The Freedom of the Will* (2012/1754). Prior to Princeton University, Edwards was a well-known minister and public speaker. Edwards defines the will as, "That by which the mind chooses any thing." It could be reasoned that the definition is contingent on the acceptance of two things: 1) the existence of mind and 2) the conscious exercise of the mind. Although the work was primarily about ethics and theological concepts of morality and good and evil, free-will clearly touches on human consciousness. Edwards argues forcefully that humans can consciously make moral choices and that there are consequences to those choices.

- *Idealism* - George Berkeley (1685-1753) was both a philosopher and an Anglican bishop in Ireland. Berkeley was a proponent of *idealism*, the notion that reality is not material, but instead is metaphysical, existing in the realm of the mind and ideas. Berkeley's idealism is both a theory of mind and an ontological theory, since it touches on the nature of reality. Some of Berkeley's most famous works include: the *Treatise Concerning the Principles of Human Knowledge* (1971/1734) and *Three Dialogues between Hylas and Philonous* (Berkeley, 1988/1713). Berkeley criticizes Descartes' mathematical support of reality along with Cartesian Dualism. Berkeley refuted the empiricist's view of the world and knowledge, as proposed by the philosopher John Locke. Berkeley's idealism was not a rejection of reality, but rather a redefinition of external reality as that which exists in the human mind and ultimately the mind of God. Although this may sound like a theological argument, Berkeley used reason to support his thesis.

The English philosopher John Locke (1632-1704) along with the French philosopher René Descartes (1596-1650) begin to point us in a new direction; namely that, human consciousness deals with awareness of one's internal thoughts and external surroundings and that the "mind" is active in the process. This is perhaps a cumbersome definition at best, since it leads us to now define what mind is. Instead of moving in that direction, I would rather address what the mind does. Simply put, the mind allows for metacognition, the ability to think about thinking (Terrace & Metcalfe, 2005). Miriam Webster defines *metacognition* as: "awareness or analysis of one's own learning or thinking processes." I would like to suggest that metacognition is a useful concept for defining consciousness ("metacognition," n.d.). I would like to suggest that metacognition is a useful concept for defining consciousness. In other words, this author defines human self-consciousness as: *the process of metacognition, being aware of one's own thinking and being able to think about the thinking of others.*

This ability to think about thinking is distinctly different from just responding to environmental stimuli. Literate humans can read newspapers and discuss the opinions on the editorial page. Illiterate humans can disagree about the thinking and conclusions of others and often do – we have a word for that too – politics! One of the characteristics that makes us uniquely human is that we have our own opinions: We rarely agree with each other in all things. Open the editorial page of any major newspaper for opposing viewpoints on topics of interest. Further example, as a reader you may be dismissing my arguments. Congratulations, you are both conscious and you are human!

Paradoxically, our legal system and the prosecuting attorney's case is predicated upon the assumption that the mind, will and emotions control the actions of individuals (an assumption that seems to bolster a theory of mind and individual responsibility). In contrast, the committed evolutionary biologist tends to be staunchly materialistic in his/her rejection of the existence of the mind. Perhaps an evolutionary biologist would not be a sound choice for a jurist, since he/she would reason that the defendant is always innocent since there is no free will!

Figure 7 is one way to think about theories of the mind. Theories of the mind can be considered as being distributed along a continuum between two disciplines of academic thought: On the one hand are the biologists who see the mind as a function of the brain, while on the other hand are the psychologists who study the mind more holistically, as being interconnected with every fiber of a person's world-view and psyche.

Figure 7 Theories of the Mind

Finally, the philosopher David Chalmers writes extensively about consciousness and argues for the development of a science of consciousness. The problem is that there is a disconnect between biologists that assert that consciousness is a materialist result of an evolutionary process, and psychologists (along with philosophers) who can neither agree on a working definition of *consciousness* nor how to study it empirically! This scientific stalemate is summarized by Chalmers (2013) who concluded, "For now, it is reasonable to hope that we may eventually have a theory of the fundamental principles connecting physical processes to conscious experience" (p. 34).

It is one thing to sit in an Introductory to Biology course at a university and hear the professor proclaim that consciousness is an evolutionary phenomenon, completely dependent on materialistic processes. It is another thing to read the scientific literature and discover that there exists no science of consciousness, or universally-held theory of conscious mind that guides social scientists.

Professor of philosophy, John D. Greenwood (2010) argues that British biologist, Thomas Huxley (1825-1895), the contemporary of Charles Darwin and defender of Darwin's theory of Descent with Modification, failed in his attempt to define consciousness. Huxley argued that our conscious and subconscious activities are the result of mechanistic external influences. Huxley gathered data (using epiphenomenology) to support the notion that in *some* cases there is evidence to support this notion, but not in all cases. Indeed, Greenwood and others argue that if all conscious and unconscious activity were the result of external stimuli, human beings would be nothing more than automatons. Professor Greenwood chooses not to take the next logical leap that if materialists and epiphenomenalists argue in support of Huxley, we are essentially abandoning human free will! Of course, free will is a cherished topic of philosophers for centuries (Markevich, 2011; Thoma, 2008), but that is a discussion for another day!

Diagraming Body, Mind and Human Self-Consciousness

Most of us will agree that to have mind, there must first be body. Some may also argue that to have self-consciousness, there must first be mind. Figure 8 shows the Relationship Between Body, Mind and Self-Consciousness.

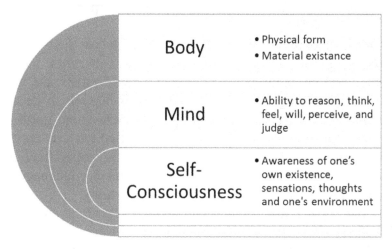

Figure 8 Relationship Between Body, Mind and Self-Consciousness

First, body is the starting point. Most of us can agree that body must exist if there is to be mind and self-awareness. If one disagrees with this statement, then we are in the area of meta-physics, which incorporates the spiritual and non-material realm.

Second, we have mind. One may argue that to have mind, there must be a brain in a body. This may be the case in certain instances, but perhaps not in all. Single-celled animals known as prokaryotes, include bacteria. The myxobacteria are single-celled animals that live in soil. What is peculiar is that the myxobacteria live in colonies and that the cells themselves specialize, as in a multi-celled creature. Cao, Dey, Vassallo and Wall (2015) discuss the following in the *Journal of Molecular Biology*:

> Like all multicellular organisms, **myxobacteria** face challenges in how to organize and maintain multicellularity. These challenges include maintaining population homeostasis, carrying out tissue repair and regulating the behavior of non-cooperators. Here, we describe the major cooperative behaviors that **myxobacteria** use: motility, predation and

development. In addition, this review emphasizes recent discoveries in the social behavior of outer membrane exchange,
wherein kin share outer membrane contents. (p. 3,709)

This is quite remarkable; molecular biologists at the University
of Wyoming are discussing single-celled myxobacteria, working
together and cooperating as a colony. The scientists use words
such as: organizing, predation, and social behavior, to describe
their function as a colony. Nowhere is the 500-pound gorilla-in-
the-room question asked: How do single-celled bacteria communicate with each other, specialize and function cooperatively as a
colony when these bacteria have neither brains nor language? Do
single-celled myxobacteria have a collective mind?

If one agrees that *mind* is defined as: the ability to reason,
think, feel, will, perceive, and judge, then we have a problem with
myxobacteria. The bacteria cooperate in a reasoned approach by
forming colonies. They sense the environment and react to it as
a colony – so they perceive and feel. They react to changes in
the environment and adjust – is this a judgment? It may be going
too far to say that the bacteria think, but thinking scientists can
see the logic in their cooperation and they do all of this without a
brain! When the brain ceases to function in a human being, we say
that the person is no longer able to function in human society. In
contrast, myxobacteria function as a society or colony with spe-
cialized functions, without any brains! Do myxobacteria bacteria
have minds? The reader can draw their own conclusion. Is there
order and apparent observable mind in the colony behavior of the
myxobacteria, perhaps there is evidence enough to argue in the
affirmative!

Third, there is self-awareness, or metacognition, the ability to
reason and think about thinking. When I taught at the university
level, one of the standard descriptors that appeared in the course
syllabus for all my classes, was that a goal of higher education is
to become a critical thinker and to develop critical thinking skills.
This does not mean that the goal is to become a skeptic such as the
philosopher Hume. The goal that I tried to teach my students was
to acquire the tools to examine the evidence when a claim is made.

The goal is to see if the evidence warrants or supports the claim. After that examination, state a conclusion based upon the evidence and the presentation of a sound argument, which either refutes or supports the original claim. This sort of higher order meta-cognitive skill is arguably something that is unique to human beings.

If these various materialist and non-materialist theories of the mind and reality seem a bit dizzying, then perhaps you are perfectly normal. Welcome to philosophy, the love (*philo*) of knowledge (*sophia*). Let us move on to a more relatable example of mind, consciousness and reality, based on a common delicacy, pizza.

Where is the Pizza?

Scientists tell us that the human brain weighs about 3 pounds. The ratio of the human brain to body mass is about 2%. Francis Crick studied the brain for the remainder of his scientific career, he and James Watson discovered DNA, but Crick (1994) could not explain how the brain works.

Scientists today can describe the dimensions and the functions of the brain, but they still have no idea how the brain works. For example, when a scientist examines the circulatory system, dye can be inserted into the blood stream. The blood can be traced and mapped as it circulates throughout the body and passes through the heart. Blood pressure can be taken and blood flow can be calculated, based on the amount of blood and heart beats per minute. In contrast, the mind and consciousness are not as simple.

When a college student is studying with a group of other students for final exams, it is not uncommon to order pizza. When pizza is ordered, it is because there is an "idea of pizza" stored somewhere in the brain. Curiously, we do not know if your idea of pizza looks like my idea of pizza. Regardless, the group of students choose their pizza toppings and they place their order for pizza delivery.

The process of stored memory, is not as simple as it seems. Human beings have a capacity for short-term and long-term memory. The students in the group that ate pizza the same day for lunch may not want to eat pizza for dinner; their short-term memory tells them that too much pizza in the same day is not a good thing. Therefore, they order lasagna. However, some other students in the study group have not had pizza for over a year (unlikely, but this is an example). We say the students that have not had pizza for a year are accessing their long-term memory of pizza[33], when they hear the word "pizza."

Such is the dilemma for the Alzheimer's patient. People suffering from Alzheimer's may be able to recall with detailed accuracy a class reunion that they attended a decade ago. However, they may not remember something they said or did (like eat pizza) in the preceding hour. Doctors can describe the effects of Alzheimer's, but they cannot trace the short-term or long-term idea of "pizza" in the brain.

Where is the pizza? For the communication theorist there is something called the semantic triangle. First, is the thing, "pizza." It is the actual food that a person holds and eats. It has substance and form; it can be tasted and smelled. Chefs can make it and compete for the tastiest pizza recipe, in a bake-off.

Second, is the symbol that represents the "pizza." It is a word on a menu. It is spelled differently in various languages, but the symbol means the same thing. The symbol is not the actual thing; it is an arbitrary sound, written word, or picture that represents the actual object. Linguists, Ogden and Richards (1923) described this relationship between an arbitrary symbol and an actual object. They called it a semantic triangle. It is the relationship between a symbol, a thought and a thing (referent).

Finally, there is the idea of "pizza." The *idea* is not a pizza and it is not a symbol. The pizza can be held (and eaten). The symbol can be written on paper and typed into a word processor. Like the actual pizza, a symbol for pizza, can have form; it can be printed on a menu, which can be held in a person's hand.

---

[33] I argue that *memory of pizza* in the brain is not the same as the word "pizza." If a person hears the word pizza for the first time but has never heard of, eaten, seen or smelled a pizza, then the word has no meaning.

The *idea of pizza* is something entirely different: It resides in the mind or consciousness of a human being. We say that the idea of pizza can be stored in short-term or long-term memory in the brain – but how do we trace it? We know that a person can see, smell, taste and swallow an actual pizza. Unlike blood, which can be traced and followed as it flows through the body, we cannot trace and follow the idea of pizza in the brain. We say that we want pizza, because it tastes delicious, or because a certain restaurant makes tasty pizza. The question remains: How do we store this information? Where is *tasty pizza* stored in the brain? Is it stored in two (or more) places? How is it accessed in the future? When we see "pizza" on a menu, how is the idea of pizza accessed in the brain to remember an idea: I enjoy pizza.

The problem with the *idea of pizza* is that it is incorporeal. An idea has no matter. It cannot be held, tasted, measured, smelled, weighed or examined in the way that a pint of blood can. This is puzzling because one may argue that if something has no mass and is invisible, it would be logical to conclude that it does not exist. However, this does not apply to the idea of pizza – it certainly does exist. The problem is further compounded by the fact that we insist that the idea of pizza is stored in our brains, however we have no clue where it is stored, how it is stored, how it is filed and indexed and how it is retrieved by short-term and long-term memory. When we look closer at the neurons in the brain through an electron microscope, we cannot see the idea of the pizza. The idea of pizza is in effect the ghost in the brain. The idea of pizza necessarily exists, but it does not exist in a corporeal state.

Here is another problem with the *idea* of pizza. We recognize it exists in incorporeal form, because for the college students who are hungry and order pizza delivery, the *idea of pizza* must necessarily exist. However, neo-Darwinism is a distinctly materialistic philosophy; it does not recognize incorporeal substances, such as the soul, or as in our example of the *idea of pizza*. Neo-Darwinism therefore, cannot explain how a group of students can order pizza from memory since there is no recognition of an incorporeal idea residing in a corporeal structure, namely the brain. Materialism cannot acknowledge the antithesis of materialism. If the materialist recognizes the "idea of pizza," that person no longer embraces materialism.

Chapter Summary

This chapter has addressed the gargantuan topic of human self-consciousness and mind, arguing that neo-Darwinism is both incomplete and inadequate in explaining the existence of human self-consciousness. At its core, neo-Darwinism is a biological theory. In contrast, topics such as human self-consciousness and mind are the purview of psychologists and philosophers. For this chapter, we chose the philosopher John Locke's definition of consciousness:

> Consciousness is the perception of what passes in a man's own mind. Can another man perceive that I am conscious of anything, when I perceive it not myself? No man's knowledge here can go beyond his experience. (Locke, 1975 / 1690)

Based on Locke's definition of consciousness, we can argue that human self-consciousness began between about 35,000 years ago, when cave-art appeared in Europe (Hudson, 2016; Valladas et al., 2001) and 3,400 B.C., when the oldest human writing was unearthed on clay tablets and stone in the ancient Assyrian city of Nineveh, located in Mosul, present-day Iraq (George, 2003). It can also be argued that human beings are unique in that only *homo sapiens* possess meta-cognition, which allows them to record and preserve ideas in writing and to think about thinking. For example, when we read a history book or an ancient text, we are thinking about the thinking of a human writer that died thousands of years before we were born! Finally, human writing allows for the codification of moral laws such as the ancient Code of Hammurabi and the Jewish 10 commandments.

In contrast, Darwin dismisses the notion that self-consciousness and higher order thinking is peculiar to mankind. First, Darwin also asserted an *a priori* conclusion: namely, that human beings are not unique among living creatures. Second, Darwin suggests that human self-consciousness is merely the result of the possession of "highly advanced intellectual faculties" which lead to the use of "a perfect language."

The field of developmental psychology, seems to be in direct opposition to Darwin's argument that self-consciousness is unique to humans. Particularly, Darwin avoids the topic of meta-cognition. Philippe Rochat (2003), a fellow of the American Academy of Child and Adolescent Psychiatry notes that there is a need to address the development of meta-cognition skills into a developmental model of child psychology and learning: "The value of the concept of meta-cognition and the point of this article is that a transformation from ordinary awareness to a more self-reflective type of consciousness is possible" (p. 5).

Another scientist who disagreed with Darwin's notion of human self-consciousness was Alfred Russel Wallace, the famous co-author of "On the tendency of species to form varieties; and on the perpetuation of varieties and species by natural means of selection" (Darwin & Wallace, 1858). Alfred Russel Wallace (1823-1913) advanced a teleological theory of evolution which included the possible outside influence of a "higher intelligence" in the universe (Jones, 2015). Francis Crick, the co-discoverer of the DNA molecule, embarked on the scientific inquiry of self-consciousness which was summarized in his book: *Astonishing Hypothesis: The Scientific Search for the Soul* (1994). Crick (1981) is known for rejecting neo-Darwinism; he concluded from his research that DNA is essentially metaphysical (as it is information) and that it is so complex that it could not originate on earth!

Finally, Philosopher Thomas Nagel (1974) in his famous article "What Is It Like to Be a Bat?," challenged the notion of evolution and scientific naturalism explaining the existence of mind. Nagel argued forcefully that while materialists acknowledge the existence of consciousness, it is logically inconsistent to fail to define *consciousness* and then use it as a basis to support materialism; this is circular reasoning. Nagel's seminal article is still debated today by students and philosophers alike.

Philosopher David Chalmers (2002) summarized the problem of consciousness in this manner:

185

There is nothing we know about more directly than consciousness, but it is extraordinarily hard to reconcile it with everything else we know. Why does it exist? What does it do? How could it possibly arise from neural processes in the brain? These questions are among the most intriguing in all of science. (p. 90)

Neo-Darwinist philosophers such as Daniel Dennett, like Huxley before him, argue forcefully to defend the materialistic view of human self-consciousness: Dennett (1991) asserts that self-consciousness arose from entirely natural processes. Philosopher Abraham Olivier (2010) disagrees with Dennett's third-party "heterophenomenological" method. Oliver argues that no matter how much data are gathered by using Dennett's methodology, "it fails ontologically," since the mind is singularly observable. This is similar to philosopher Thomas Nagel's (1974) argument in his famous article "What Is It Like to Be a Bat? Nagel's seminal argument is so forceful, that it continues to be the discussed and challenged, by philosophers today (Bearn, 2015; Doggett & Stoljar, 2010; Levin, 2007).

Both the 18th century philosopher David Hume (1748, 1955) and Daniel Dennett (1991) wrestle with the same question: Is it possible for anyone to know with certainty what goes on in the mind of another human being? Are colors created in the mind, or does the mind observe colors through the eyes and then categorize variations and shades of colors from a composite database? Put another way: Is the red color that you see, the same color red that I see? The argument can be extended to any color or combination of colors.

The American Heritage Dictionary defines *mind* as: "The human consciousness that originates in the brain and is manifested, esp. in thought, perceptions, feeling, will. Memory, or imagination" (Morris, 1982). Unfortunately, there is no consensus of definition of what *mind* is, when comparing between various academic sources. Mind seems to be a metaphysical reality, that defies the traditional heuristic scientific method of observation.

What is the best way to address the question: What is mind? The French mathematician and Philosopher René Descartes (1596-1650) pioneered a theory of the mind which is referred to as mind/body dualism. Descartes asserted what he called an indubitable truth, *cogito ergo sum*, translated from the Latin as: "I think, therefore I am." (Kant, Gregor, & Timmermann, 1785 / 2012). By stating this truth, Descartes was saying that it is my ability to think (my consciousness or self-awareness) that defines my existence. Descartes' theory, which is also referred to as *Cartesian Dualism* (Deary, 2005), has not been widely accepted.

To this day, the debate has not been settled as to what the mind is. There are many modern theories of the mind which have been proposed.

- *Dualism* – A theory of the mind advanced by the French philosopher René Descartes (1596-1650). Descartes argued that the mind and body are two distinct entities, connected by the pituitary gland in the brain. The body is material and the mind has no physical substance. (Blom, 1978; Feldman, 1986; Pearl, 1977)
- *Functionalism* – *The Stanford Encyclopedia of Philosophy* states:
  Functionalism, in the philosophy of mind is the doctrine that what makes something a mental state of a particular type does not depend on its internal constitution, but rather on the way it functions, or the role it plays, in the system of which it is a part. This doctrine is rooted in Aristotle's conception of the soul, and has antecedents in Hobbes's conception of the mind as a "calculating machine." (Levin, 2016)
- *Parallelism* - Gottfried Wilhelm von Leibniz' (1646-1716). There is no mind-body interaction strictly speaking, but only a non-causal relationship of harmony, parallelism, or correspondence between mind and body (Kulstad & Carlin, 2013).
- *Epiphenominalism* - Attributed to Thomas Huxley (1825– 1895) and William James (1842-1910). Epiphenomenalism is the view that mental events are caused by physical events in the brain, but have no effects upon any physical events (Greenwood, 2010).

- *Free Will* – Free will is not so much a definition of mind, as it is a definition of the exercise or function of the human mind. According to theologian and philosopher, Jonathan Edwards (2012/1754), *Free Will* is: "That by which the mind chooses any thing." It could be reasoned that the definition is contingent on the acceptance of two things: 1) the existence of mind and 2) the conscious exercise of the mind (J. Edwards, 1804).
- *Idealism* - George Berkeley (1685-1753) The notion that reality is not material, but instead is metaphysical, existing in the realm of the mind and ideas. Berkeley's idealism is both a theory of mind and an ontological theory, since it touches on the nature of reality (Berkeley, 1971/1734, 1988/1713).

One of the things that makes us uniquely human is our ability to experience, *metacognition*, in other words, humans can think about thinking (Fox & Riconscente, 2008; Schmitt & Sha, 2009; Terrace & Metcalfe, 2005). Examples of metacognition include: 1) reading a newspaper and thinking about what a reporter wrote and 2) attending a conference where various speakers make presentations on a variety of topics.

Finally, the philosopher David Chalmers summarizes the scientific stalemate between biologists and psychologists. On the one hand, biologists assert that consciousness is a materialist result of an evolutionary process. In contrast, psychologists (who study human behavior) cannot agree on a working definition of *consciousness*, or how to study it empirically! Chalmers (2013) concludes: "For now, it is reasonable to hope that we may eventually have a theory of the fundamental principles connecting physical processes to conscious experience" (p. 34). According to the scientific literature, there is no science of consciousness or universal theory of conscious mind that guides social scientists. This author argues that there is a relationship between body, mind and self-consciousness.

In the allegory of the pizza-in-the-mind, I argue that we all agree that there is such a thing that we call pizza. We may even agree that the *idea of pizza* may reside in the brain or the mind, but we also must conclude that when the human brain is examined scientifically, the pizza cannot be located.

The word "pizza" can be recorded on a magnetic tape, or located on a computer hard drive, in the form of a .wav file. At present the mysterious .wav file in the brain (or mind) has not been located, and the *pizza* file in the brain continues to evade empirical observation by neuro scientists and social scientist alike. Even the famous scientist Francis Crick, who discovered DNA with Watson, was not able to explain what precisely consciousness is (Crick, 1994).

VIII. Conclusion

*Alice asked the Cheshire Cat, who was
sitting in a tree, "What road do I take?"
The cat asked, "Where do you want to go?"
"I don't know," Alice answered.
"Then," said the cat, "it really doesn't matter, does it?"*
Lewis Carroll (1865 / 2017),
Alices' Adventures in Wonderland

Like the Cheshire Cat in the famous Lewis Carroll children's classic, the question remains: "Where do you want to go?"

Most of the readers of this book will have heard of Charles Darwin and a theory called *evolution*, which has been attributed to him, before they read this book. However, most readers probably were not taught a few of these facts in school:

- **Darwin disliked and strongly objected to the term** *evolution*. The term *evolution* was initially promoted and advanced by the philosopher Herbert Spencer (1866, p. Preface to Eng. Ed.). Darwin only used the term *evolution*, in his 6th and final edition of *On the Origin of Species* (Darwin, 1876).
- **Darwin openly referred to the "Creator" as the source of life.** The first edition of *On the Origin of Species* (Darwin, 1859, p. 490) does not use the term *Creator* in the last sentence of the book. Editions 2 through 6 have the phrase

191

"breathed by the Creator," in the final sentence of *On the Origin of Species*.

- **The Earth does not change slowly over time**. Modern day geology has refuted Darwin's argument that the Earth changes very slowly over time. Uniformitarianism has been replaced by catastrophism (Luis W. Alvarez, 1987; W. Alvarez, 2008; Benton, 2003; Berggren & Van Couvering, 1984; Morell, 1993).

- **Some non-religious philosophers and scientists disagree with Darwin**. Some modern philosophers do not agree that evolution and neo-Darwinism are facts; the most famous of these philosophers is perhaps Karl Popper (1976). Philosopher Jerry Fodor and professor of cognitive science Massimo Piattelli-Palmarini offer a powerful criticism of Darwin's theories in their book: *What Darwin Got Wrong* (2010). The book *Uncommon Dissent* (Dembski, 2004), is an edited book with writings from religious and non-religious scientists and philosophers who disagree with Darwin. The narrative, or story of neo-Darwinism, has been taught to children during their educational years in elementary, high school years and beyond. As a narrative, much of what has been propped up as science, is nothing more than scientific story-telling. The result is that there is a scientific leap-of-faith required to accept the narrative, since the story is riddled with enormous gaps between the scientifically verifiable empirical data. These gaps are often filled in by narratives or stories which sound scientific but are not backed up by empirical data.

- **Darwin never explained the origin of life**. Even though Darwin wrote a book called: *On the Origin of Species by Means of Natural Selection: Or, the Preservation of Favored Races in the Struggle for Life* (Darwin, 1859), this book and later editions never explained how life began. Today, neo-Darwinism still does not explain how life began. Spontaneous generation of life from non-life has never been observed by scientists (Phillips, 2010). Francis Crick (1981), the co-discover of DNA, concluded that DNA is so complex that it could not have been formed by natural causes on Earth. Crick's conclusion is that life on planet Earth was seeded by some other civilization in the universe, a theory called *panspermia* (Napier, 2004).

- **The origin of DNA has not been explained.** Neo-Darwinism cannot explain the natural formation of DNA (Ball, 2013; Morange, 2008). There is no scientific theory that has ever both explained and observed the formation of DNA, naturally in the field. Many scientists believe DNA was not formed by natural processes on Earth, but was brought from other worlds. Scientists refer to the seeding of life from other worlds as *panspermia* (Crick, 1981; Waldrop, 2011; Wesson, 2010; White, 1998; C. Wickramasinghe, 2003; Chandra Wickramasinghe, 2011).

- **All life is homochiral at the molecular level** (Barron, 2008; Klabunovskii, 2012). This supports the notion that at the fundamental molecular level, life is not random. All life is *homochiral* (Crick, 1981); it is built upon left-handed amino acids, without exception! This is documented in the scientific journal: *Chirality* (Bonner, 2000).

- **The formation of bacteria are a mystery.** The formation of the first living thing, commonly referred to as bacteria ("Prokaryote," 2013) has never been explained. Bacteria are still present today, they have not changed in hundreds of millions of years (Altermann & Kazmierczak, 2003; Hazen, Roedder, Powers, Vreeland, & Rosenweig, 2001). They are the most stable form of life on Earth. Some bacteria have been brought back to life after being frozen for 250 million years! (Knight, 2001).

- **The formation of a nucleus in a single-cell cannot be explained.** This has never been observed in the field. The first form of life on Earth were bacteria, with no nucleus. Later single-celled life, called *eukaryotes*, formed nuclei ("Eukaryotes and the First Multicellular Life Forms," 2013). Scientists have observed (Embley & Martin, 2006), "the evolutionary gap between prokaryotes and eukaryotes is now deeper, and the nature of the host that acquired the mitochondrion more obscure, than ever before." The term *protist* refers to the classification, Kingdom Protista, which includes single-celled living things with a nucleus. (Margulis, 2005; Sharma & Shukla, 2009).

- **Development of Multi-cellularity has never been explained**. Single-celled living things are called *prokaryotes*. Multi-celled living things are made up of cells that are as much as 500 times the size of prokaryotes (Tortora et al., 2010, p. 101). The cells in multi-celled living things are called *eukaryotes*[34]. The theory of endosymbiosis (Margulis, 1998), which tries to explain the transition from single-celled life to multi-celled life is a narrative: It has never been directly observed and verified by scientists (Poole & Penny, 2007).
- **Neo-Darwinism cannot explain the Three Barriers to Life.**

Bacteria
- Barrier 1: Emergence of first life, 3.8-3.5 billion years ago.
- Prokaryotes (bacteria), the first life on Earth.
- Natural selection cannot explain beginning of life and first DNA code.

Protists
- Barrier 2: Emergence of protists 2.5 billion years ago.
- Eukaryote Protists (Single-celled), genus amoeba
- SET theory, has no explanation for DNA in protist cells, 500x larger!

Multicelled Eukaryotes
- Barrier 3: Emergence of multicellularity 1.5 billion years ago.
- Eukaryote (Multi-celled); Cambrian Explosion (525 mya)
- There is no accepted theory to explain multicellularity.

---

[34] Single-celled life can exist without a nucleus; these living things are called bacteria or prokaryotes. Eukaryotes have a nucleus and can be 500 times larger than a prokaryote (Tortora et al., 2010, p. 101). Eukaryotes can be either single-celled (i.e. amoeba) or multi-celled (all other life). Eukaryotes are highly complex, when compared to prokaryotes. Eukaryotes have special structures called *organalles* that prokaryotes do not.

- **Evolution cannot explain the formation of the human mind**. Evolution also cannot explain the ability of the human mind to think about thinking; this is called *metacognition*. Neo-Darwinism and modern evolutionary theory is, at its core a materialistic theory that attempts to explain the origin of species, based upon naturally observed phenomena. The mind (like the information contained in DNA) is essentially without body: It is *incorporeal,* without material form. It is a fallacy to attempt to explain something that is metaphysical (mind) with a materialistic theory.

In his work, *Principia Ethica*, English philosopher G.E. Moore (1903) raises the question that is debated to this very day: Why should *good* necessarily exist naturally? [35]

> . . .the naturalistic fallacy is a fallacy, or, in other words, that we are all aware of a certain simple quality, which (and not anything else) is what we mainly mean by the term good; and (2) to shew [*sic*] that not one, but many different things, possess this property.

Moore terms this dilemma, the *naturalistic fallacy*. In short, if we recognize that a certain action or behavior is good and then we recognize that a different behavior is also good, by what natural phenomena do we measure the quality of goodness of one act versus another? Who is to say that one action is *good-er* than another action? How is one to recognize that there is a universal measuring scale of *good-ness*, that is both empirically observable and universally acknowledged?

So as the Cheshire Cat begs the question, "Where do you want to go?" In other words, where do you want to go with this information? In summary, Darwin did not initially introduce a theory called *evolution*, indeed he despised the term which was advanced by philosopher Herbert Spencer. Darwin suggested that life was

---

[35] Here, I only briefly touch on the topic of *ethics*. If I am able in a future edition of this work to address this topic more completely, I will.

originally, "breathed by the Creator" in the last sentence of editions 2 through 6 of *On the Origin of Species*. Evolution cannot explain the beginning of life, the formation of DNA, the formation of the first single-celled life form (bacteria), or the emergence of the first multi-celled living thing. Darwin did not know that 100% of life is *homochiral*: amino acids in living things are left-handed. This means that life is not random! Darwin was wrong about the geology of the Earth. Life on Earth is not shaped by slow processes over time: Life has been impacted over millennia by numerous major cataclysms. Finally, evolution is not an empirically verifiable scientific theory: Evolution or neo-Darwinism is rather a scientific narrative – a story told by academics and educators.

Where do you want to go from here? What story do you want to believe? The Cat begs the question. Will you be a critical thinker and seek out answers? If you don't know, then I suppose, as the Cheshire Cat concludes, "it really doesn't matter, does it?"

IX. Recommended Reading

In the Introduction of this book I wrote the following, in response to the question: Why did you write this book?

> Colleagues have asked me: What gives you the right to criticize evolutionary theory? After all, they say, I have neither a background in biology or the physical sciences. My response is straightforward. Evolution ceased to be a biological theory a long time ago. It is a metatheory, or put simply, a theory of theories. Today, evolution is imbedded in the following literature (and more): biology, geology, paleontology, systematics, genetics, population genetics, astronomy, anthropology, sociology, psychology, ethics and my field of communication. Ironically, there are frequent gaps of empirical evidence in the field of biological evolution. Where gaps exist, there is a generous use of deductive reasoning and narrative, which are used to glue the story together. Narrative becomes the super glue that fills in holes where empirical evidence is lacking, beginning with biology! Therefore, I have written this book to challenge the paradigm, or what Dr. Jeremy Narby (1998) calls, "the current orthodoxy" (p. 145). Get ready for a ride!

Hopefully, you have enjoyed the ride and the journey. Now it is time for me to reveal my bias. I do believe that there is a God and I do believe that the universe is intrinsically teleological, in other words, created by a Designer. I also believe that Charles Darwin also acknowledged the same, since he wrote, "There is grandeur in this view of life, with its several powers, having been originally breathed by the Creator into a few forms or into one" (Darwin, 1861, 1866, 1869, 1876). The dates here reflect the second, third, fourth and final editions of Darwin's, *On the origin of species by means of natural selection, or the preservation of favoured races in the struggle for life*.

Darwin was a practicing Christian, when he began his famous voyage upon the *Beagle*, to the Galapagos Islands, As Darwin describes it,

> During these two years I was led to think much about religion. Whilst on board the *Beagle* I was quite orthodox, and I remember being heartily laughed at by several of the officers (though themselves orthodox) for quoting the Bible as an unanswerable authority on some point of morality. . . I gradually came to disbelieve in Christianity as a divine revelation . . . This disbelief crept over me at a very slow rate, but was at last complete. (Barlow, 2005, pp. 71-72)

Darwin was familiar with the teleological argument for the existence of God, which was advanced by the theologian and phi-losopher, William Paley (1743-1805). Paley stated his argument in the first paragraph of his book *Natural Theology*[36] as such:

> In crossing a heath, suppose I pitched my foot against a *stone*, and were asked how the stone came to be there, I might possibly answer, that, for any thing I knew to the contrary, it had lain there for ever [*sic*]: nor would it per-haps be very easy to shew the absurdity of this answer. But suppose I had found a *watch* upon the ground, and it should be enquired how the watch happened to be in that place, I

---

[36] This book was originally published in 1802 and was updated many times by its author, William Paley, D.D. Paley, himself published updated editions of this book, and it continues to be republished today with historical background and biographical information about the author.

should hardly think of the answer which I had before given, that, for anything I knew, the watch might have always been there. Yet why should not this answer serve for the watch, as well as for the stone? Why is it not as admissible in the second case, as in the first? For this reason, and for no other, viz. that, when we come to inspect the watch, we perceive (what we could not discover in the stone) that its several parts are framed and put together for a purpose, e.g. that they are so formed and adjusted as to produce motion, and that motion so regulated as to point out the hour of the day; that, if the several parts had been differently shaped from what they are, of a different size from what they are, or placed after any other manner, or in any other order, than that in which they are placed, either no motion at all would have been carried on in the machine, or none which would have answered the use, that is now served by it. . . This mechanism being observed (it requires indeed an examination of the instrument, and perhaps some previous knowledge of the subject, to perceive and understand it; but being once understood), the inference, we think, is inevitable; that the watch must have had a maker; that there must have existed, at some time and at some place or other, an artificer or artificers who formed it for the purpose which we find it actually to answer; who comprehended its construction, and designed its use. (Paley, 1802/2006, pp. 7-8)

Paley's argument has since become known as the argument by design, or what philosophers refer to as the teleological argument. This refers to those sets of arguments and facts that lead to the conclusion that the universe implies an order and as such there is a Creator or a Designer who is behind the order of the universe. This argument is so powerful and profound that it has been studied in universities around the world as the field of natural theology.

Darwin, of course, was very familiar with Paley's argument. Darwin was required to read Paley's books for his B.A. degree at Cambridge, which he completed in 1831 (Van Whye, 2009). Darwin comments on his final exams at Cambridge:

In order to pass the B.A. examination, it was, also necessary to get up Paley's *Evidences of Christianity*, and his *Moral Philosophy*. This was done in a thorough manner, and I am convinced that I could have written out the whole of the *Evidences* with perfect correctness, but not of course in the clear language of Paley. The logic of this book and as I may add of his *Natural Theology* gave me as much delight as did Euclid. (Barlow, 2005, pp. 50-51)

Darwin continues, later in his biography, and discusses Paley's arguments, "The old argument by design in nature, as given by Paley, which formerly seemed to me so conclusive, fails, now that the law of natural selection has been discovered" (Barlow, 2005, p. 73).

It is curious that Darwin seems to pivot and almost contradict his earlier logic. Darwin himself criticized Spencer in his deductive approach to science; Darwin initially rejected the terms evolution and law of evolution which were coined by Spencer. I covered this subject matter in detail in the first chapter of this book and simply point the reader back to that chapter, to refresh, and reflect upon Darwin's criticism of the philosopher Herbert Spencer. In Darwin's rejection of Paley's argument, which he made later in life, he now almost conveniently pulls Spencer's logic out of the hat, to swat away Paley's argumentation from his *Natural Theology*.

A continuation of a discussion of the argument by design and the field of natural theology is beyond the scope of this book. Many volumes have been written on these topics over the last 200 years. Both natural theology and natural philosophy were prominent fields of study at one time. Today, natural philosophy is referred to as science.

At this point, I must conclude, although I may be persuaded to continue this topic with a companion study guide, at some future date. For the present, it has been pressed upon me to not leave the reader hanging, but to at least suggest some additional sources, to aid the reader on the topics of teleology, evolutionary theory, scientific discovery and theology. Take note that sometimes I give guidance on what books should be read prior to reading the more difficult works on this list. I also make note of certain books which are linked in subject matter to other books on this list.

Annotated Reading List

Alvarez, W. (2008). T. Rex and the Crater of Doom. Princeton, New Jersey, Princeton University Press.
Professor of Geology Walter Alvarez, at University of California, Berkeley, caused a scientific revolution (Kuhn, *The Structure of Scientific Revolutions*), by shaking the field of geology and earth sciences away from gradualism to catastrophism. The evidence was found in Mexico, at Chicxulub, where a giant meteorite fell about 65 million years ago. Alvarez caused a scientific revolution (read: Kuhn, *The Structure of Scientific Revolutions*). The Chicxulub meteorite is credited with the extinction of the dinosaurs.

Benton, M. J. (2003). When Life Nearly Died: the greatest mass extinction of all time. New York, Thames & Hudson.
From the publisher, "Michael Benton is Professor of Vertebrate Paleontology and Head of the Department of Earth Sciences at the University of Bristol. He has written over forty books, many of them standard technical works and textbooks, as well as popular books about dinosaurs and the history of life." Everything you ever wanted to know about catastrophism and the history of the Earth; this is the primary introductory source to this topic. Read this book along with Alvarez, *T. Rex and the Crater of Doom*; along with Ward, *On Methuselah's Trail: living fossils and the great extinctions*. Particularly interesting are chapters 10 and 11 which discuss the end-Permian mass extinction, which occurred 251 million years ago. According to Benton "close studies of the Meishan section in China have shown that 95% of species died out at that time, or within the following 800,000 years" (p. 255).

Barlow, N., Ed. (2005). The Autobiography of Charles Darwin 1809-1882. New York, W. W. Norton & Company.
Charles Darwin's autobiography; this is primary source material. A telling book which shows how Darwin's thinking changed over the years. Darwin is strikingly self-aware of his state of mind through the different stages of his life. He also comments frequently about his discussions with other scientists and scholars during his lifetime. A must-read to understand Darwin, in the *zeitgeist* of his lifetime.

Behe, M. J. (1998). Darwin's Black Box: the biochemical challenge to evolution, Free Press.
The book that started all the uproar in the scientific community. Behe is a professor of Biological Science at Lehigh University and a outstanding microbiologist. He has dared to venture from the dominant paradigm of neo-Darwinism and assert the teleological argument by design. This is a modern-day continuation of Paley's argument for a Designer. Whereas, Paley began his argument with a watch, Behe begins his argument with a living cell. Behe coins the term: *irreducible complexity*, which has lit a fire in the scientific community. Behe asserts, "By *irreducibly complex* I mean a single system composed of several well-matched, interacting parts that contribute to the basic function, wherein the removal of any one of the parts causes the system to effectively cease functioning. An irreducibly complex system cannot be produced directly (that is, by continuously improving the initial function, which continues to work by the same mechanism) by slight, successive modifications of a precursor system, because any precursor to an irreducibly complex system that is missing a part is by definition nonfunctional." (p. 39)

Behe, M. J. (2007). The Edge of Evolution: The Search for the Limits of Darwinism. New York, Free Press.
This is a follow-up to Michael Behe's earlier work *Darwin's Black Box*. On the back sleeve cover, Jeffrey M Schwartz, M.D. writes, "In crystal-clear prose Behe systematically shreds the central dogma of atheistic science, the doctrine of the random

universe. This book, like the natural phenomena it so elegantly describes, shows the unmistakable signs of a very deep intelligence at work."

Brockman, J., Ed. (2006). Intelligent Thought: science versus the intelligent design movement. New York, Vintage Books.
This book is an edited volume with chapters from leading scientific atheists who are pushing back against intelligent design. The curious title of the book suggests that there is a fight between science and intelligent design. The truth is that the teleological argument has existed for millennia whereas, modern day science is a recent development, that sprang forth from the 17th century Age of Enlightenment, beginning with the writings of Francis Bacon and the British Royal Society. One of my favorite chapters is titled "Evolution and Ethics" by Stephen Pinker. In that chapter, Pinker acknowledges, "It's true that science cannot provide us with moral principles." He then goes on to take a swipe at religion by adding: "But neither can religion. An understanding of morality is to be found through secular moral reasoning and lies in fundamental facts about the human condition, not the dictates of a supreme deity" (p. 143). Pinker glosses over the fact that human moral reasoning brought us Karl Marx and communism, which resulted in close to 100 million deaths in the 20th century with world leaders such as, Mao, Stalin, Lenin, Pol Pot and others. We can also throw in the benefits of the Age of Enlightenment, which could not curtail two World Wars! This book should be read simultaneously with *The soul of science: Christian faith and natural philosophy.*

Darwin, C. (1876/1998). The Origin of Species: By means of natural selection or The preservation of favored Races in the struggle for life. New York, The Modern Library.
Difficult to read and long, this is the original source material – a must-read. You can still walk into most well stocked bookstores and buy this off the shelf. The last sentence reads, "There is a grandeur in life, with its several powers, having been originally breathed by the Creator into a few forms or into one; and that,

whilst this planet has gone cycling on according to the fixed law of gravity, from so simple a beginning endless forms most beautiful and most wonderful have been, are being evolved" (p. 649).

Dembski, W. A. (2004). Uncommon dissent: intellectuals who find Darwinism unconvincing. Wilmington, Del., ISI Books.
William A. Dembski is Research Professor in Philosophy at Southwestern Seminary in Ft. Worth. This is perhaps the most powerful and well-articulated counter argument to the modern doctrine of neo-Darwinism. This is an edited volume with articles from various professors, academics and intellectuals who choose to think critically about neo-Darwinism. This book is highly recommended.

D'Souza, D. (2011). What's so great about Christianity. New York, NY, MJF Books.
This Christian apologetic work is a tour de force. I especially enjoyed Chapter 13: Paley Was Right: Evolution and the Argument by Design. Another personal favorite was Chapter 21: The Ghost in the Machine: Why Man is More Than Matter.

Fodor, J. A. and M. Piattelli-Palmarini (2010). What Darwin Got Wrong. New York, Farrar, Straus and Giroux.
"Jerry Fodor is a professor of philosophy and cognitive science at Rutgers University." Massimo Piattelli-Palmarini has an academic background in biophysics and molecular biology and is a professor of cognitive science at the University of Arizona. This book is both a scientific and philosophical criticism of the fundamental assumptions upon which modern neo-Darwinism rests. Well researched with exceptional sourcing and indexing. This could be a key critical text in the academic classroom. From the back cover, "*What Darwin Got Wrong* is a remarkable book, one that dares to challenge the theory of natural selection as an explanation for how evolution works – a devastating critique not in the name of religion but in the name of good science."

Fortey, R. A. (2012). Horseshoe Crabs and Velvet Worms: the story of the animals and plants that time has left behind. New York, Alfred A. Knopf.

Richard Fortey was a senior paleontologist at the Natural History Museum in London. Detailed and elegantly written with many photos of fossils and their modern ancestors which live today, with no change at all. A few examples are the: nautilus, horseshoe crab, velvet worm, jellyfish, sponges, ginkgo biloba trees, Australian lungfish, lamprey, turtle, platypus, and the hearty enduring cockroach.

Kuhn, T. S. (1962/1996). The Structure of Scientific Revolutions. Chicago, IL, University of Chicago Press.

Thomas Kuhn was a physicist, historian and philosopher of science. Hailed as one of the ten greatest scientific philosophy works of the 20th century. Don't even attempt reading this book until first reading a book like Mosley and Lynch's, *The Story of Science*. After reading *The Structure of Scientific Revolutions* you will understand that science operates within parameters of agreement between scholars, or what Kuhn calls, *paradigms*. When a major scientific discovery takes place (such as Newtonian physics) the scientific community shifts; this is what Kuhn calls a scientific revolution or a paradigm shift. Kuhn gives many examples of paradigm shifts. Walter Alvarez's book which is in this suggested reading list, is a modern example of a paradigm shift.

Magee, B. (2001). The Story of Philosophy. New York, DK Publishing, Inc.

This is a great introductory book to the study of *philosophy*, which is defined by the Greek as, "love of wisdom." Philosophy is the most fundamental of all sciences; it is the platform from which all fields of scientific enquiry stand and develop from. This could be a starting point for anyone interested in studying philosophy. It begins with the Greek philosophers and continues with the major thinkers, to the modern age. The book is filled with 4 color illustrations and pictures on almost every page.

Miller, K. and B. Stein (2008). Expelled: No Intelligence Allowed. USA, Premise Media Corporation.
This is a movie, not a book! If you want to take a break from reading and wish to watch an entertaining documentary with Ben Stein, which explores evolution and intelligent design, then look no further. Ben Stein's primary thesis is that there is no academic freedom on college campuses to challenge evolution. Stein interviews professors who have been blacklisted and delves into the dark side of evolution, by uncovering the history of the eugenics movement. Includes a discussion guide. Length: 1 hr., 30 min.

Mosley, M. and J. Lynch (2010). The Story of Science: Power, proof and passion. London, Octopus Publishing Group.
If you enjoy reading about scientific discoveries and the process of discovery and research, this is the book for you! It is plentifully supplied with color illustrations and photographs on almost every page. This should be considered an introductory popular text. Read it and then place it on your coffee table to see who will gravitate towards it to discuss the topics included. Organized in sections: cosmos, matter, life, body and mind.

Narby, J. (1998). The Cosmic Serpent: DNA and the origins of knowledge. New York, Jeremy P. Tarcher/Putnam.
Jeremy Narby, Ph.D. has a doctorate in anthropology from Stanford University. He is on the forefront of scholars who dare to challenge the entrenched thinking of neo-Darwinism which permeates college campuses today. Narby's primary thesis is that the universe is not the result of natural random forces but is in fact minded.

National Academy of Sciences and Institute of Medicine. (2008). Science, Evolution, and Creationism. Washington, D.C., The National Academies Press.
At this writing, this small book can be downloaded in .pdf format for free. It is interesting that proponents of neo-Darwinism attempt to frame scientists and intellectuals who reject Darwin

as creationists. Nothing could be further from the truth. The truth is that there are scientists, intellectuals and philosophers who are atheists, but also reject Darwinism. This book shows that there is a battle going on for the minds and souls of school-aged children. As dedicated scientists and university professors are beginning to push back on Darwinism, entrenched groups such as the National Academy of Sciences are resisting the emerging research from microbiology, geology, physics, philosophy and other fields.

Paley, W. (1802/2006). Natural Theology or Evidence of the Existence and Attributes of the Deity, collected from the appearances of nature. Oxford, Oxford University Press.
Paley was a theologian and philosopher, trained at Christ College, Cambridge, England. Read *Natural Theology*, with an updated introduction. Imagine Charles Darwin reading this at Cambridge between 1828 and 1831. A classic which has affected philosophy and theology for 200 years! Darwin read an earlier version of this work, to pass his B.A. exam in 1831.

Pearcey, N. and C. B. Thaxton (1994). The Soul of Science: Christian faith and natural philosophy. Wheaton, Ill., Crossway Books.
This book makes the argument that modern day science was built upon the shoulders and discoveries of many of the greatest past scientists, who were professing followers of Christ. "Christians were not a marginalized minority . . .The truth is that we cannot really understand a Newton, a Descartes or a Cuvier without delving into the religious and philosophical ideas that drove their scientific work" (p. xii).

Rosen, S., Ed. (2007). Philosophy 101: Selections from the Works of the Western World's Greatest Thinkers. New York, Gramercy Books.
If you are new to philosophy, don't start with this book. Read an introduction to philosophy book like Bryan Magee's, *The Story of Philosophy*, first. If you still have the desire to learn more, this

would be a great place to continue. These are selections from the great western philosophers and scientists. This is primary source material, so you may need other resources and guide material, to help you navigate through it. Books like this are typically not read cover to cover, but in sections. Germane to the topic of evolution would be Part Six: Philosophy of Science. In addition, Part Two, addresses religion; Part Four discusses metaphysics.

Schroeder, G. L. (2001). The Hidden Face of God: science reveals the ultimate truth. New York, Free Press.
Author, Gerald L. Schroeder earned his Ph.D. from Massachusetts Institute of Technology; he has worked in both physics and biology. Schroder has written other books which also discuss the unity between science and religion. Highlights include Chapter 4: The Orderly Cells of Life, where Schroeder discusses bacteria appearing 3.6 billion years ago and the fact that Francis Crick (an atheist) considered the beginning of life to be caused by other than natural forces. Chapter 9: Thinking About Thinking: Taping into the Conscious Mind of the Universe, is also highly recommended. This book is an amazing combination of science, philosophy and metaphysics. A must-read on this list!

Ward, P. D. (1992). On Methuselah's Trail: living fossils and the great extinctions. New York, W.H. Freeman.
Peter Douglas Ward is Professor of Geological Sciences and Curator of Invertebrates, Thomas Burke Museum at the University of Washington in Seattle. Read this book after reading Alvarez, *T. Rex and the Crater of Doom*. There are chapters on flat clams, the nautilus and ammonites, the horseshoe crab, plants and the famous coelacanth; this was a fish that was once thought to be extinct and 100 million years old!

References

Altermann, W., & Kazmierczak, J. (2003). Archean microfossils: a reappraisal of early life on Earth. *Research in Microbiology, 154*(9), 611. doi:10.1016/j.resmic.2003.08.006

Alvarez, L. W. (1987). Mass extinctions caused by large bolide impacts. *Physics Today, 40*(7), 24.

Alvarez, L. W., Alvarez, W., Asaro, F., & Michel, H. V. (1980). Extraterrestrial cause for the Cretaceous-Tertiary extinction. *Science, 208*(4448), 1095-1108. doi:10.1126/science.208. 4448.109

Alvarez, W. (2008). *T. rex and the crater of doom* (New Princeton science library paperback ed.). Princeton, New Jersey: Princeton University Press.

Anderson, O. (2007). CHARLES LYELL, UNIFORMITARIANISM, AND INTERPRETIVE PRINCIPLES. *Zygon: Journal of Religion & Science, 42*(2), 449-462. doi:10.1111/j.1467-9744. 2007.00449.x

Arbib, M. A. (2014). Co-evolution of human consciousness and language (revisited). *Journal of Integrative Neuroscience, 13*(2), 187-200. doi:10.1142/S021963521440007X

Arthur, W. (2011). Searching for evo-devo's Holy Grail: the nature of developmental variation. *Evolution & Development, 13*(5), 405-407. doi:10.1111/j.1525-142X.2011.00498.x

Ball, P. (2013). DNA: Celebrate the unknowns. *Nature, 496*(7446), 419-420. doi:10.1038/496419a

Baluška, F. (2009). Cell-Cell Channels, Viruses, and Evolution. *Annals of the New York Academy of Sciences, 1178*(1), 106-119. doi:10.1111/j.1749-6632.2009.04995.x

Barlow, N. (Ed.) (2005). *The autobiography of Charles Darwin 1809-1882.* New York: W. W. Norton & Company.

Barnosky, A. D., Matzke, N., Tomiya, S., Wogan, G. O. U., Swartz, B., Quental, T. B., . . . Ferrer, E. A. (2011). Has the Earth's sixth mass extinction already arrived? *Nature, 471*(7336), 51-57. doi:10.1038/nature09678

Barron, L. D. (2007). Chemistry: Compliments from Lord Kelvin. *Nature, 446*(7135), 505-506. doi:10.1038/446505a

Barron, L. D. (2008). Chirality and Life. *Space Science Reviews, 135*(1-4), 187-201. doi:10.1007/s11214-007-9254-7

Bearn, G. (2015). Bats? Again? William James, Consciousness, and Our Insipid Existence (Vol. 29, pp. 522-546).

Behe, M. J. (1998). *Darwin's Black Box: The Biochemical Challenge to Evolution*: Free Press.

Behe, M. J. (2007). *The Edge of Evolution: The Search for the Limits of Darwinism.* New York: Free Press.

Benton, M. J. (2003). *When life nearly died: the greatest mass extinction of all time.* New York: Thames & Hudson.

Berggren, W. A., & Van Couvering, J. A. (1984). *Catastrophes and earth history : the new uniformitarianism.* Princeton, N.J.: Princeton University Press.

Berkeley, G. (1971/1734). *A treatise concerning the principles of human knowledge, 1734.* Menston,: Scolar Press.

Berkeley, G. (1988/1713). *Three dialogues between Hylas and Philonous.* Buffalo, N.Y.: Prometheus Books.

Berney, C., Fahrni, J., & Pawlowski, J. (2004). How many novel eukaryotic 'kingdoms'? Pitfalls and limitations of environmental DNA surveys. *BMC Biology, 2*, 13-13.

Berra, T. M. (1990). *Evolution and the myth of creationism : a basic guide to the facts in the evolution debate.* Stanford, Calif.: Stanford University Press.

Black, F. W., & Black, I. L. (1982). ANTERIOR-POSTERIOR LOCUS OF LESION AND PERSONALITY: SUPPORT

FOR THE CAUDALITY HYPOTHESIS. *Journal of Clinical Psychology, 38*(3), 468-477.

Blatner, A. (2004). THE DEVELOPMENTAL NATURE OF CONSCIOUSNESS TRANSFORMATION. *ReVision, 26*(4), 2-7.

Blom, J. J. (1978). *Descartes: His Moral Philosophy and Psychology*. New York: New York University Press.

Boiteux, S., & Jinks-Robertson, S. (2013). DNA Repair Mechanisms and the Bypass of DNA Damage in Saccharomyces cerevisiae. *Genetics, 193*(4), 1025-1064. doi:10.1534/genetics.112.145219

Bolhuis, J. J., Brown, G. R., Richardson, R. C., & Laland, K. N. (2011). Darwin in Mind: New Opportunities for Evolutionary Psychology. *PLoS Biology, 9*(7), 1-8. doi:10.1371/journal. pbio.1001109

Bonner, W. A. (2000). Parity violation and the evolution of biomolecular homochirality. *Chirality, 12*(3), 114-126. doi:10.1002/ (SICI)1520-636X(2000)12:3<114::AID-CHIR3>3.0.CO;2-N

Brahic, C. (2014). Oldest hand stencil found in Indonesia. *New Scientist, 224*(2990), 10-10.

Brand, U., Posenato, R., Came, R., Affek, H., Angiolini, L., Azmy, K., & Farabegoli, E. (2012). The end-Permian mass extinction: A rapid volcanic CO_2 and CH_4-climatic catastrophe. *Chemical Geology, 322-323*, 121-144. doi:10.1016/j.chemgeo.2012.06.015

Brooks, K. (2012). Sirius Passet, Greenland and the Cambrian Explosion. *Geology Today, 28*(4), 144-146. doi:10.1111/j.1365-2451.2012.00842.x

Cao, P., Dey, A., Vassallo, C. N., & Wall, D. (2015). How Myxobacteria Cooperate. *Journal of Molecular Biology, 427*(23), 3709-3721. doi:10.1016/j.jmb.2015.07.022

Carroll, L. (1865 / 2017). *Alice's Adventures in Wonderland*: AmazonClassics.

Case, E. (2008). TEACHING TAXONOMY: How Many Kingdoms? *American Biology Teacher (National Association of Biology Teachers), 70*(8), 472-477.

Casmir, F. L. (Ed.) (1994). *Building Communication Theories: A Socio/Cultural Approach*. Hillsdale, NJ: Lawrence Erlbaum Associates.

Catastrophism. (2013)Columbia Electronic Encyclopedia (6th ed.): Columbia University Press. Retrieved from http://0-search. ebscohost.com.library.regent.edu/login.aspx?direct=true&db=a 2h&AN=39050904&site=ehost-live.

Cavalier-Smith, T. (1998). A revised six-kingdom system of life. *Biological Reviews, 73*(3), 203.

Cells within cells: An extraordinary claim with extraordinary evidence. (2012). Retrieved from understandingscience.org website: http://undsci.berkeley.edu/lessons/pdfs/endosymbiosis.pdf

Chalmers, D. J. (2002). the puzzle of conscious experience. *Scientific American Special Edition, 12*(1), 90-100.

Chalmers, D. J. (2013). How can we construct a science of consciousness? *Annals of the New York Academy of Sciences, 1303*(1), 25-35. doi:10.1111/nyas.12166

Chevance, F. F. V., & Hughes, K. T. (2008). Coordinating assembly of a bacterial macromolecular machine. *Nature Reviews Microbiology, 6*(6), 455-465. doi:10.1038/nrmicro1887

Chudley, A. E. (2000). Genetic landmarks through philately – Crick, Watson and Wilkins: the scientists behind DNA structure. *Clinical Genetics, 57*(1), 26-28. doi:10.1034/j.1399-0004.2000.570104.x

Clary, R., & Wandersee, J. (2011). Krakatoa Erupts! *Science Teacher, 78*(9), 42-47.

Clough, M. P., Colbert, J. T., Kelly, C. D., Rice, J. W., & Warner, D. A. (2010). The Theory of Evolution is Not an Explanation for the Origin of Life. *Evolution: Education and Outreach, 3*(2), 141+.

Code of Hammurabi. (2017). *Encyclopædia Britannica*. Retrieved from Encyclopædia Britannica website: https://www.britannica.com/topic/Code-of-Hammurabi consciousness. (2017). *Encyclopædia Britannica*: Encyclopædia Britannica, inc.

Cotner, S., & Moore, R. (2011). *Arguing for evolution : an encyclopedia for understanding science*. Santa Barbara, Calif.: Greenwood.

Crick, F. (1981). *Life itself : its origin and nature*. New York: Simon and Schuster.

Crick, F. (1994). *The astonishing hypothesis : the scientific search for the soul*. New York: Scribner ; Maxwell Macmillan International.

Curtis, T. P., Sloan, W. T., & Scannell, J. W. (2002). Estimating prokaryotic diversity and its limits. *Proceedings of the National Academy of Sciences, 99*(16), 10494-10499. doi:10.1073/pnas.142680199

Da Xiong, H., Hai Yan, W., Zhi Liang, J., An Fu, H., & Yu Fen, Z. (2010). Amino Acid Homochirality may be Linked to the Origin of Phosphate-Based Life. *Journal of Molecular Evolution, 70*(6), 572-582. doi:10.1007/s00239-010-9353-z

Daly, H. E. (2000). What Neo-Darwinism Does Not Explain: Response to Trombulak and Matter and McPherson. *Conservation Biology, 14*(4), 1206-1207. doi:10.1046/j.1523-1739.2000.00020.x

Danovaro, R., Dell'Anno, A., Pusceddu, A., Gambi, C., Heiner, I., & Kristensen, R. M. (2010). The first metazoa living in permanently anoxicconditions. *BMC Biology, 8*, 30-39. doi:10.1186/1741-7007-8-30

Darwin, C. (1859). *On the Origin of Species by Means of Natural Selection: Or, the Preservation of Favored Races in the Struggle for Life*. London,: J. Murray.

Darwin, C. (1860). *On the Origin of species by means of natural selection, or the preservation of favoured races in the struggle for life* (2nd ed.). London: John Murray.

Darwin, C. (1861). *On the origin of species by means of natural selection, or the preservation of favoured races in the struggle for life* (3rd ed.). London: John Murray.

Darwin, C. (1863a). 18 April 1863, Letter to Athenæum. Retrieved from Darwin Correspondence Project website: http://www.darwinproject.ac.uk/entry-4108

Darwin, C. (1863b). The Doctrine of Heterogeny and Modification of Species. *Athenaeum. Journal of Literature, Science, and the Fine Arts, 1852*(25), 554-555.

Darwin, C. (1866). *On the origin of species by means of natural selection, or the preservation of favoured races in the struggle for life* (4th ed.). London: John Murray.

Darwin, C. (1869). *On the origin of species by means of natural selection, or the preservation of favoured races in the struggle for life* (5th ed.). London: John Murray.

Darwin, C. (1871). Feb 1, 1871 - Letter to J.D. Hooker. Retrieved from Darwin Correspondence Project website: http://www.darwinproject.ac.uk/entry-7471

Darwin, C. (1871/2004). *The Descent of Man: And Selection in Relation to Sex*. New York: Barnes & Noble, Inc.

Darwin, C. (1876). *The origin of species by means of natural selection, or the preservation of favoured races in the struggle for life. London* (6th ed.). London: John Murray.

Darwin, C. (1876/1998). *The Origin of Species: By means of natural selection or The preservation of favorored Races in the struggle for life* (6th ed.). New York: The Modern Library.

Darwin, C. (1889). *The Origin of Species: By Means of Natural Selection Or The Preservation of Favored Races In The Struggle For Life* (6th ed. Vol. 1). New York: D. Appleton & Company.

Darwin, C., & Darwin, F. (1887). *The life and letters of Charles Darwin*. New York,: D. Appleton and company.

Darwin, C., & Wallace, A. R. (1858). On the tendency of species to form varieties; and on the perpetuation of varieties and species by natural means of selection. *Journal of the Proceedings of The Linnean Society, 3*, 45-62.

Dawkins, R. (1996). *The blind watchmaker : why the evidence of evolution reveals a universe without design*. New York: Norton.

Dawkins, R. (2006). *The God delusion*. Boston: Houghton Mifflin Co.

Deary, V. (2005). Explaining the unexplained? Overcoming the distortions of a dualist understanding of medically unexplained illness. *Journal of Mental Health, 14*(3), 213-221. doi:10.1080/09638230500136605

Dembski, W. A. (2004). *Uncommon dissent: intellectuals who find Darwinism unconvincing*. Wilmington, Del.: ISI Books.

Dennett, D. C. (1991). *Consciousness explained* (1st ed.). Boston: Little, Brown and Co.

Dennett, D. C. (1996). *Kinds of minds : toward an understanding of consciousness* (1st ed.). New York, NY: Basic Books.

Der Giezen, M. V. (2011). Mitochondria and the Rise of Eukaryotes. *Bioscience, 61*(8), 594-601. doi:10.1525/bio.2011.61.8.5

Di Giulio, M. (2011). The Last Universal Common Ancestor (LUCA) and the Ancestors of Archaea and Bacteria were Progenotes.

Journal of Molecular Evolution, 72(1), 119-126. doi:10.1007/s00239-010-9407-2

Dobzhansky, T. (1973). Nothing in Biology Makes Sense Except in the Light of Evolution. *American Biology Teacher, 35*, 125-129.

Doggett, T., & Stoljar, D. (2010). DOES NAGEL'S FOOTNOTE ELEVEN SOLVE THE MIND-BODY PROBLEM? *Philosophical Issues, 20*(1), 125-143. doi:10.1111/j.1533-6077.2010.00184.x

Dott, R. H. J. (2000). Serendipity and Stan Tyler's Precambrian Gunflint Fossils. *The Outcrop*, 25-26. Retrieved from Department of Geoscience, University of Wisconsin-Madison website: http://www.geology.wisc.edu/outcrop/00/index.html

Durant, W. (2005). *The story of philosophy; the lives and opinions of the greater philosophers of the Western World.* New York: Simon & Schuster Paperbacks.

Edwards, C. L. (1900). Animal Myths and Their Origin. *The Journal of American Folklore, 13*(48), 33-43.

Edwards, J. (1804). *A careful and strict inquiry into the modern prevailing notions of that freedom of will, which is supposed to be essential to moral agency, virtue and vice, reward and punishment, praise and blame.* Albany: Printed for and sold by Whiting, Backus & Whiting, no. 45, Statestreet: sold also by them at their stores in Schenectady, Utica and Canandaigua.

Edwards, J. (2012/1754). *Freedom of the will.* Mineola, N.Y.: Dover Publications.

Edwards, P. (Ed.) (1967). *The Encyclopedia of Philosophy* (Vol. 7-8). New York: Macmillan.

Elfstrom, G. (2009). After the double helix ... what? *Journal of the Alabama Academy of Science, 80*, 233+.

Embley, T. M., & Martin, W. (2006). Eukaryotic evolution, changes and challenges. *Nature, 440*(7084), 623-630.

Emeline, A. V., Otroshchenko, V. A., Ryabchuk, V. K., & Serpone, N. (2003). Abiogenesis and photostimulated heterogeneous reactions in the interstellar medium and on primitive earth: Relevance to the genesis of life. *Journal of Photochemistry and Photobiology, 3*(3), 203-224.

Eukaryotes and the First Multicellular Life Forms. (2013). Retrieved from Smithsonian National Museum of Natural History website:

http://paleobiology.si.edu/geotime/main/htmlversion/protero
zoic3.html

Feldman, F. (1986). *A Cartesian Introduction to Philosophy*. New York: McGraw-Hill.

Ferrari, M., Pinard, A., & Runions, K. (2001). Piaget's Framework for a Scientific Study of Consciousness. *Human Development (0018716X), 44*(4), 195-213. doi:10.1159/000057059

Flavell, J. H. (1996). PIAGET'S LEGACY. *Psychological Science (0956-7976), 7*(4), 200-203.

Fodor, J. A., & Piattelli-Palmarini, M. (2010). *What Darwin got wrong* (1st American ed.). New York: Farrar, Straus and Giroux.

Follmann, H., & Brownson, C. (2009). Darwin's warm little pond revisited: from molecules to the origin of life. *Naturwissenschaften, 96*(11), 1265-1292. doi:10.1007/s00114-009-0602-1

Fox, E., & Riconscente, M. (2008). Metacognition and Self-Regulation in James, Piaget, and Vygotsky *Educational Psychology Review, 20*, 373–389. doi:10.1007/s10648-008-9079-2

Friedrich, W. L. (2000). *Fire in the Sea: The Santorini Volcano: Natural History and the Legend of Atlantis* (A. R. McBirney, Trans.). Cambridge: Cambridge University Press.

Furgason, J. M., & Bahassi, E. M. (2013). Targeting DNA repair mechanisms in cancer. *Pharmacology & Therapeutics, 137*(3), 298-308. doi:10.1016/j.pharmthera.2012.10.009

Futuyma, D. J. (1986). *Evolutionary biology* (2nd ed.). Sunderland, Mass.: Sinauer Associates.

Futuyma, D. J. (2009). *Evolution* (2nd ed.). Sunderland, Mass.: Sinauer Associates.

Gallup. (2006). American Beliefs: Evolution vs. Bible's Explanation of Human Origins. Retrieved from http://www.gallup.com/poll/21811/american-beliefs-evolution-vs-bibles-explanation-human-origins.aspx?version=print

George, A. R. (2003). *The epic of Gilgamesh : the Babylonian epic poem and other texts in Akkadian and Sumerian*. London; New York: Penguin Books.

Gould, S. J. (1977). *Ever since Darwin : reflections in natural history* (1st ed.). New York: W. W. Norton & Company.

Gould, S. J. (1983). *Hen's teeth and horse's toes* (1st ed.). New York: Norton.

Gould, S. J. (2007). *Punctuated equilibrium* (1st pbk. ed.). Cambridge, Mass.: Belknap Press of Harvard University Press.

Greenwood, J. (2010). Whistles, bells, and cogs in machines: Thomas Huxley and epiphenomenalism. *Journal of the History of the Behavioral Sciences, 46*(3), 276-299.

Handwerk, B. (2012). New Underwater Finds Raise Questions About Flood Myths. *national Geographic News, 2013*(August 5). Retrieved from National Geographic website: http://news.nationalgeographic.com/news/2002/05/0528_020528_sunk-encities.html

Haught, J. F. (2009). THEOLOGY, EVOLUTION, AND THE HUMAN MIND: HOW MUCH CAN BIOLOGY EXPLAIN? *Zygon: Journal of Religion & Science, 44*(4), 921-931. doi:10.1111/j.1467-9744.2009.01041.x

Hazen, R. M., Roedder, E., Powers, D. W., Vreeland, R. H., & Rosenweig, W. D. (2001). How old are bacteria from the Permian age? *Nature, 411*(6834), 155.

Hudson, H. (Writer). (2016). Finding Altamira [Film]. In L. Bickford (Producer). Spain.

Hume, D. (1748, 1955). *An Inquiry Concerning Human Understanding*. Indianapolis: The Liberal Arts Press, Inc.

Isaac, S., & Michael, W. (1995). *Handbook in Research and Evaluation* (3rd ed.). San Diego, CA: EdITS Publishers.

Iyama, T., & Wilson, D. M. (2013). DNA repair mechanisms in dividing and non-dividing cells. *DNA Repair, 12*(8), 620-636. doi:10.1016/j.dnarep.2013.04.015

James Hutton. (2002). *Microsoft Encarta*. Redmond, WA: Microsoft Corporation.

Jones, H. (2015). The Vision of Alfred Russel Wallace. *Journal for Spiritual & Consciousness Studies, 38*(1), 17-24.

Kant, I., Gregor, M. J., & Timmermann, J. (1785 / 2012). *Groundwork of the metaphysics of morals* (Revised edition / ed.). Cambridge: Cambridge University Press.

Kauffman, S. A. (2006). Intelligent Design, Science or Not? In J. Brockman (Ed.), *Intelligent Thought: Science Versus the Intelligent Design Movement* (pp. 169-178). New York: Vintage Books.

King, C. (1877). Catastrophism and Evolution. *The American Naturalist, 11*(8), 449-470.

Klabunovskii, E. (2012). Homochirality and its significance for biosphere and the origin of life theory. *Russian Journal of Organic Chemistry, 48*(7), 881-901. doi:10.1134/S1070428012070019

Knight, J. (2001). THE IMMORTALS. *New Scientist, 170*(2288), 36.

Kohut, A. (2009). *Scientific Achievements Less Prominent Than a Decade Ago PUBLIC PRAISES SCIENCE; SCIENTISTS FAULT PUBLIC, MEDIA*. Retrieved from Washington, DC: http://www.people-press.org/files/legacy-pdf/528.pdf

Krakatoa. (2001)Microsoft Encarta. Redmond, WA: Microsoft Corporation.

Kuhn, T. S. (1962/1996). *The structure of scientific revolutions* (3rd ed.). Chicago, IL: University of Chicago Press.

Kulstad, M., & Carlin, L. (2013). *Leibniz's Philosophy of Mind* E. N. Zalta (Ed.) *The Stanford Encyclopedia of Philosophy* Retrieved from https://plato.stanford.edu/archives/win2013/entries/leibniz-mind/

Kutschera, U. (2009). Symbiogenesis, natural selection, and the dynamic Earth. *Theory in Biosciences, 128*(3), 191-203. doi:10.1007/s12064-009-0065-0

Lal, A. K. (2008). Origin of Life. *Astrophysics & Space Science, 317*(3/4), 267-278. doi:10.1007/s10509-008-9876-6

Lamarck, J.-B. (1809/1914). *Zoological Philosophy. An Exposition with Regard to the Natural History of Animals* (H. Elliot, Trans.). London: Macmillan.

Lane, N. (2009). Biodiversity: On the origin of bar codes. *Nature, 462*(7271), 272-274. doi:10.1038/462272a

Lane, N., Allen, J. F., & Martin, W. (2010). How did LUCA make a living? Chemiosmosis in the origin of life. *BioEssays, 32*(4), 271-280. doi:10.1002/bies.200900131

Lane, N., & Martin, W. (2010). The energetics of genome complexity. *Nature, 467*(7318), 929-934. doi:10.1038/nature09486

Langone, J., Stutz, B., & Gianopoulos, A. (2006). *Theories for everything : an illustrated history of science from the invention of numbers to string theory* (1st ed.). Washington, D.C.: National Geographic.

Lendon, B. (2013). 'Ice tsunamis' sweep into homes. Retrieved from http://www.cnn.com/2013/05/13/us/ice-tsunamis

Levin, J. (2007). NAGEL VS. NAGEL ON THE NATURE OF PHENOMENAL CONCEPTS. *Ratio, 20*(3), 293-307. doi:10.1111/j.1467-9329.2007.00366.x

Levin, J. (2016). *Functionalism* E. N. Zalta (Ed.) *The Stanford Encyclopedia of Philosophy* Retrieved from https://plato.stanford.edu/archives/win2016/entries/functionalism/

Lewis, R. W. (1988). Theory and the Fact of Evolution. *Creation Evolution Journal, 8*(1), 34-37.

Littlejohn, S. W. (2002). *Theories of Human Communication* (7th ed.). Albuquerque: Wadsworth Thompson Learning.

Locke, J. (1975 / 1690). *An Essay Concerning Human Understanding* (P. H. Nidditch Ed.). Oxford: Clarendon Press.

Lynch, M. (2005). Intelligent design or intellectual laziness? *Nature, 435*, 276.

Lynn Margulis. (2011). *The Telegraph*. Retrieved from The Telegraph website: http://www.telegraph.co.uk/news/obituaries/science-obituaries/8954456/Lynn-Margulis.html

Magee, B. (2001). *The story of philosophy*. New York: DK Publishing, Inc.

Maier, B., Chen, I., Dubnau, D., & Sheetz, M. P. (2004). DNA transport into Bacillus subtilis requires proton motive force to generate large molecular forces. *Nature Structural & Molecular Biology, 11*(7), 643-649. doi:10.1038/nsmb783

Maloney, P. C., Kashket, E. R., & Wilson, T. H. (1974). A protonmotive force drives ATP synthesis in bacteria. *Proceedings of the National Academy of Sciences of the United States of America, 71*(10), 3896-3900.

Malthus, T. (1798). *An Essay on the Principle of Population*. London: J Jonson.

Margulis, L. (1970). *Origin of eukaryotic cells; evidence and research implications for a theory of the origin and evolution of microbial, plant, and animal cells on the Precambrian earth*. New Haven,: Yale University Press.

Margulis, L. (1998). *Symbiotic planet : a new look at evolution* (1st ed.). New York: Basic Books.

Margulis, L. (2005). The Names of Life. *American Scientist, 93*(4), 290-290.

Margulis, L., & Knoll, A. H. (2005). Elso Sterrenberg Barghoorn, Jr. *Biographical Memoirs, 87*, 92-109.

Margulis, L., & Sagan, D. (2002). *Acquiring genomes : a theory of the origins of species* (1st ed.). New York, NY: Basic Books.

Markevich, V. V. (2011). Is Freedom of Will an Invention of the Evolution? V. V. Markevich. *Cultural-Historical Psychology* (1), 42-48.

Martin, W., Baross, J., Kelley, D., & Russell, M. J. (2008). Hydrothermal vents and the origin of life. *Nature Reviews Microbiology, 6*(11), 805-814. doi:10.1038/nrmicro1991

Martin, W., & Embley, T. M. (2004). Evolutionary biology: Early evolution comes full circle. *Nature, 431*(7005), 134-137.

Maynard Smith, J., & Szathmáry, E. r. (1995). *The major transitions in evolution.* Oxford; New York: W.H. Freeman Spektrum.

Mayr, E. (1999). *Systematics and the origin of species, from the viewpoint of a zoologist* (1st Harvard University Press pbk. ed.). Cambridge, Mass.: Harvard University Press.

Mayr, E. (2001). *What evolution is.* New York: Basic Books.

Mende, D. R., Sunagawa, S., Zeller, G., & Bork, P. (2013). Accurate and universal delineation of prokaryotic species. *Nature Methods, 10*(9), 881-884. doi:10.1038/nmeth.2575

metacognition. (n.d.). Retrieved from Merriam-Webster.com website: http://www.dictionary.com/browse/metacognition?s=t

mind. (n.d.). *Dictionary.com Unabridged.* Retrieved from Dictionary.com website: http://www.dictionary.com/browse/mind

Misconceptions about Evolution. (2012). Retrieved from http://evolution.berkeley.edu/evolibrary/misconceptions_about_evolution.pdf

Moore, G. E. (1903). *Principia ethica.* Cambridge,: At the University press.

Morange, M. (2008). *Life explained.* New Haven: Yale University Press.

Morell, V. (1993). How lethal was the K-T impact? *Science, 261*(5128), 1518.

Morris, W. (1982). *The American Heritage Dictionary* (2nd college ed.). Boston: Houghton Mifflin.

Mosley, M., & Lynch, J. (2010). *The Story of Science: Power, proof and passion.* London: Octopus Publishing Group.

Müller, G. B. (2007). Evo–devo: extending the evolutionary synthesis. *Nature Reviews Genetics, 8*(12), 943-949. doi:10.1038/nrg2219

Nagel, T. (1974). What Is It Like to Be a Bat? *The Philosophical Review, 83*(4), 435-450.

Nagel, T. (2012). *Mind & Cosmos: Why the Materialist Neo-Darwinian Conception of Nature is Almost Certainly False.* Oxford: Oxford University Press.

Napier, W. M. (2004). A mechanism for interstellar panspermia. *Monthly Notices of the Royal Astronomical Society, 348*(1), 46-51. doi:10.1111/j.1365-2966.2004.07287.x

Narby, J. (1998). *The cosmic serpent : DNA and the origins of knowledge* (1st Jeremy P. Tarcher/Putnam ed.). New York: Jeremy P. Tarcher/Putnam.

National Academy of Sciences and Institute of Medicine. (2008). *Science, Evolution, and Creationism.* Washington, D.C.: The National Academies Press.

Newton, I. (1687/1803). *The Mathematical Principles of Natural Philosophy* (A. Motte, Trans.). London: H. D. Symonds.

Nida-Rümelin, J. (2014). Thomas Nagel: Mind and Cosmos. Why the Materialist, Neo-Darwinian Conception is Almost Certainly False. *Journal for General Philosophy of Science, 45*(2), 403-406. doi:10.1007/s10838-014-9262-8

NSTA. (2013). NSTA Position Statement: The Teaching of Evolution. Retrieved from http://www.nsta.org/pdfs/PositionStatement_Evolution.pdf

Ogden, C. K., & Richards, I. A. (1923). *The Meaning of Meaning.* London: Kegan, Paul, Trench, Trubner.

Okasha, S. (2012). Population Genetics. In E. N. Zalta (Ed.), The Stanford Encyclopedia of Philosophy. Stanford, CA: The Metaphysics Research Lab, Standford University. Retrieved from http://plato.stanford.edu/archives/fall2012/entries/population-genetics/.

Olivier, A. (2010). The possibility of a science of consciousness Critical reflections on Dennett and Merleau-Ponty. *South African Journal of Philosophy, 29*(2), 104-116.

Ollis, A. A., Manning, M., Held, K. G., & Postle, K. (2009). Cytoplasmic membrane protonmotive force energizes periplasmic interactions between ExbD and TonB. *Molecular Microbiology, 73*(3), 466-481. doi:10.1111/j.1365-2958.2009.06785.x

Paley, W. (1802/2006). *Natural Theology or Evidence of the Existence and Attributes of the Deity, collected from the appearances of nature*. Oxford: Oxford University Press.

Pälike, H. (2013). Impact and Extinction. *Science, 339*(655). doi:10.1126/science.1233948

Pawlowski, J. (2013). The new micro-kingdoms of eukaryotes (Vol. 11, pp. 1-3): BioMed Central.

Pearl, L. (1977). *Descartes*. Boston: Twayne Publishers.

Penny, D., & Poole, A. (1999). The nature of the last universal common ancestor. *Curr Opin Genet Dev, 9*(6), 672-677.

Penrose, R. (Ed.) (2015). *Consciousness and the universe*: Cosmology Science Publishers.

Peretó, J., Bada, J. L., & Lazcano, A. (2009). Charles Darwin and the Origin of Life. *Origins of Life and Evolution of Biospheres: The Journal of the International Astrobiology Society, 39*(5). doi:10.1007/s11084-009-9172-7

Phillips, M. L. (2010). The Origins Divide: Reconciling Views on How Life Began. *Bioscience, 60*(9), 675-680. doi:10.1525/bio.2010.60.9.3

Piechocinska, B. (2016). Evidence-based physics beyond materialism. *Physics Essays,29*(4),508-512. doi:10.4006/0836-1398-29.4.508

Plato. (360 B.C.E.). *Timaeus* Retrieved from http://classics.mit.edu/Plato/timaeus.html

Poole, A., & Penny, D. (2007). Eukaryote evolution: Engulfed by speculation. *Nature, 447*(7147), 913-913.

Popper, K. R. (1976). *Unended quest : an intellectual autobiography* ([Revised ed.). [London]: Fontana.

Popper, K. R. (1982). *Unended quest : an intellectual autobiography* ([Revised ed.). La Salle: Open Court.

Powell, E. A. (2014). North America's Oldest Petroglyphs. *Archaeology, 67*(1), 28-28.

Prokaryote. (2013). *Encyclopædia Britannica.* Retrieved from Encyclopædia Britannica website: http://www.britannica.com/EBchecked/topic/478531/prokaryote

Prothero, D. R. (2007a). *Evolution: What the fossils say and why it matters.* New York: Columbia University Press.

Prothero, D. R. (2007b). *Evolution: What the Fossils Say and Why it Matters.* New York: Columbia University Press.

Puhvel, J. (2017). cuneiform. Retrieved from Encyclopædia Britannica website: https://www.britannica.com/topic/cuneiform

Rasmussen, B., Fletcher, I. R., Brocks, J. J., & Kilburn, M. R. (2008). Reassessing the first appearance of eukaryotes and cyanobacteria. *Nature, 455*(7216), 1101-1104. doi:10.1038/nature07381

Rasmussen, S., Chen, L., Deamer, D., Krakauer, D. C., Packard, N. H., Stadler, P. F., & Bedau, M. A. (2004). Transitions from Nonliving to Living Matter. *Science, 303*(5660).

Reimold, W. U. (2003). Impact cratering: a young discipline coming of age. *South African Journal of Science, 99*(7/8), 307-308.

Reimold, W. U. (2007). Revolutions in the Earth Sciences: Continental Drift, Impact and other Catastrophes. *South African Journal of Geology, 110*(1), 2-46.

Retallack, G. J., Dunn, K. L., & Saxby, J. (2013). Problematic Mesoproterozoic fossil Horodyskia from Glacier National Park, Montana, USA. *Precambrian Research, 226*, 125-142. doi:10.1016/j.precamres.2012.12.005

Robertson, M. (2004). Francis Crick, 1916-2004: Francis Harry Compton Crick, who with James Watson and Maurice Wilkins was awarded the Nobel Prize in 1962 for elucidating the structure of DNA and its significance in biological information transfer, died on 28 July at the age of 88. *Bioscience, 54*(9), 808+.

Robinson, W. (2015). *Epiphenomenalism* E. N. Zalta (Ed.) *The Stanford Encyclopedia of Philosophy* Retrieved from https://plato.stanford.edu/archives/fall2015/entries/epiphenomenalism

Rochat, P. (2003). Five levels of self-awareness as they unfold early in life. *Consciousness and Cognition, 12*, 717–731. doi:10.1016/S1053-8100(03)00081-3

Rogers, K. (2013). mitochondrion. *Encyclopædia Britannica*. Retrieved from http://www.britannica.com/EBchecked/topic/386130/mitochondrion

Ruiz-Trillo, I., Burger, G., Holland, P. W. H., King, N., Lang, B. F., Roger, A. J., & Gray, M. W. (2007). The origins of multi-cellularity: a multi-taxon genome initiative. *Trends in Genetics, 23*(3), 113-118. doi:10.1016/j.tig.2007.01.005

Ruse, M. (2004, January). Natural Selection vs. Intelligent Design. *USA Today Magazine, 132*, 32-34.

Russell, M. J., Hall, A. J., & Martin, W. (2010). Serpentinization as a source of energy at the origin of life *Geobiology, 8*(5), 355-371. doi:10.1111/j.1472-4669.2010.00249.x

Sagan, L. (1967). On the origin of mitosing cells. *J Theor Biol, 14*(3), 255-274.

Sankaran, N. (2012). How the discovery of ribozymes cast RNA in the roles of both chicken and egg in origin-of-life theories. *Studies in History & Philosophy of Biological & Biomedical Sciences, 43*(4), 741-750. doi:10.1016/j.shpsc.2012.06.002

Sapp, J., Carrapiço, F., & Zolotonosov, M. (2002). Symbiogenesis: The Hidden Face of Constantin Merezhkowsky. *History & Philosophy of the Life Sciences, 24*(3/4), 413-440.

Schabas, M. (2001). David Hume on Experimental Natural Philosophy, Money, and Fluids. *History of Political Economy, 33*(3), 411-435.

Schmitt, M. C., & Sha, S. (2009). The developmental nature of meta-cognition and the relationship between knowledge and control over time. *Journal of Research in Reading, 32*(2), 254-271. doi:10.1111/j.1467-9817.2008.01388.x

Schopf, J. W. (1993). Microfossils of the Early Archean Apex chert: New evidence of the antiquity of life. *Science, 260*(5108), 640.

Schopf, J. W. (1999). *Cradle of life : the discovery of earth's earliest fossils*. Princeton, N.J.: Princeton University Press.

Schopf, J. W., & Kudryavtsev, A. B. (2010). A renaissance in studies of ancient life. *Geology Today, 26*(4), 140-145. doi:10.1111/j.1365-2451.2010.00760.x

Schopf, J. W., Kudryavtsev, A. B., Agresti, D. G., Wdowiak, T. J., & Czaja, A. D. (2002). Laser-Raman imagery of Earth's earliest fossils. *Nature, 416*(6876), 73-76.

Schroder, W. (1999). Were noctilucent clouds caused by the Krakatoa eruption? A case study of the research problems. *80*, 2081.

Schroeder, G. L. (2001). *The hidden face of God : science reveals the ultimate truth.* New York: Free Press.

Searle, J. R., Dennett, D. C., & Chalmers, D. J. (1997). *The mystery of consciousness* (1st ed.). New York: New York Review of Books. semiotics. (n.d.). *Dictionary.com Unabridged.* Retrieved from http://www.dictionary.com/browse/semiotics

Sharma, M., & Shukla, Y. (2009). The evolution and distribution of life in the Precambrian eon-Global perspective and the Indian record. *Journal of Biosciences, 34*(5), 765-776. doi:10.1007/s12038-009-0065-8

Sheehan, R. J., & Rode, S. (1999). On Scientific Narrative: Stories of Light by Newton and Einstein. *Journal of Business & Technical Communication, 13*(3), 336-358. doi:10.1177/105065199901300306

Smith, C. M. (2011). *The fact of evolution.* Amherst, N.Y.: Prometheus Books.

Sommer, R. J. (2009). The future of evo–devo: model systems and evolutionary theory. *Nature Reviews Genetics, 10*(6), 416-422. doi:10.1038/nrg2567

Spencer, H. (1852). The Development Hypothesis. *The Leader.*

Spencer, H. (1855). *The Principles of Psychology.* London: Longman, Brown, Green and Longmans.

Spencer, H. (1862/1898). *First Principles* (4th ed.). New York: D. Appleton & Co.

Spencer, H. (1866). *The Principles of Biology.* New York: D. Appleton and Company.

Spencer, H. (1891). *Essays: Scientific, Political, & Speculative* Vol. 1. (pp. 525).

Terrace, H. S., & Metcalfe, J. (2005). *The missing link in cognition : origins of self-reflective consciousness*. Oxford; New York: Oxford University Press.

Thoma, N. (2008). The Question of Free Will, Determinism and Responsibility in the Social Sciences. *History & Philosophy of Psychology, 10*(1), 9-15.

Tortora, G. J., Funke, B. R., & Case, C. L. (2010). *Microbiology : an introduction* (10th ed.). San Francisco, CA: Pearson Benjamin Cummings.

Trajstman, A. C., & Watterson, G. A. (1972). A note on a first passage probability found in population genetic models. *Theor Popul Biol, 3*(4), 396-403.

Trombulak, S. C. (2000). Misunderstanding Neo-Darwinism: a Reaction to Daly. *Conservation Biology, 14*(4), 1202-1203. doi:10.1046/j.1523-1739.2000.99558.x

Tyler, S. A., & Barghoorn, E. S. (1954). Occurrence of Structurally Preserved Plants in Pre-Cambrian Rocks of the Canadian Shield. *Science, 119*(3096), 606-608. doi:10.1126/science.119.3096.606

Uniformitarianism. (2013)Columbia Electronic Encyclopedia (6th ed.): Columbia University Press. Retrieved from http://0-search. ebscohost.com.library.regent.edu/login.aspx?direct=true&db=a 2h&AN=39037552&site=ehost-live.

Urrutia-Fucugauchi, J., & Perez-Cruz, L. (2011). Buried impact basins, the evolution of planetary surfaces and the Chicxulub multi-ring crater. *Geology Today, 27*(6), 220-225. doi:10.1111/ j.1365-2451.2011.00814.x

Valladas, H., Clottes, J., Geneste, J. M., Garcia, M. A., Arnold, M., Cachier, H., & Tisnerat-Laborde, N. (2001). Evolution of prehistoric cave art. *Nature, 413*(6855), 479.

Van Whye, J. (2009). Charles Darwin's Cambridge Life 1828-1831. *Journal of Cambridge Studies, 4*(4), 2-13.

Wadsworth, B. J. (2004). *Piaget's theory of cognitive and affective development* (Classic ed.). Boston: Pearson/A and B.

Wagler, R. (2011). The Anthropocene Mass Extinction: An Emerging Curriculum Theme for Science Educators. *American Biology Teacher (National Association of Biology Teachers), 73*(2), 78-83. doi:10.1525/abt.2011.73.2.5

Wainwright, M. (2003). A Microbiologist looks at Panspermia. *Astrophysics & Space Science, 285*(2), 563-570.

Waldrop, M. M. (2011). The search for alien intelligence: SETI is dead ? long live SETI. *Nature, 475*(7357), 442-444. doi:10.1038/475442a

Wallace, A. R. (1853). *Palm trees of the Amazon and their uses.* London: J. Van Voorst.

Wallace, A. R. (1853/1889). *A narrative of travels on the Amazon and Rio Negro : with an account of the native tribes, and observations of the climate, geology, and natural history of the Amazon Valley / by Alfred Russel Wallace; with a biographical introduction by the editor* (2d ed. ed.). London: Ward, Lock.

Wallace, A. R. (1895). *Natural selection and tropical nature* (2 ed.). London and New York,: Macmillan and Co.

Walter, C. (2015, January). The First Artists. *National Geographic,* 32-57.

Ward, P. D., & Brownlee, D. (2004). *Rare earth: why complex life is uncommon in the universe.* New York: Copernicus.

Watson, J. D. (1968). *The double helix: a personal account of the discovery of the structure of DNA.* London,: Weidenfeld & Nicolson.

Watson, J. D., & Crick, F. (1953). Molecular structure of nucleic acids: a structure for deoxyribose nucleic acid. *Nature, 171,* 737-738.

Watterson, G. A. (1975). On the number of segregating sites in genetical models without recombination. *Theor Popul Biol, 7*(2), 256-276.

Webb, E. J., Campbell, D. T., Schwartz, R. D., & Lee, S. (2000). *Unobtrusive measures* (Rev. ed.). Thousand Oaks, Calif.: Sage Publications.

Webster, N. (1828/1983). *American Dictionary of the English Language.* San Francisco, CA: The Foundation for American Christian Education.

Wesson, P. (2010). Panspermia, Past and Present: Astrophysical and Biophysical Conditions for the Dissemination of Life in Space. *Space Science Reviews, 156*(1-4), 239-252. doi:10.1007/s11214-010-9671-x

Westerlund, J. F., & Fairbanks, D. J. (2010). Gregor Mendel's classic paper and the nature of science in genetics courses. *Hereditas, 147*(6), 293-303. doi:10.1111/j.1601-5223.2010.02199.x

White, M. (1998). *Life out there : the truth of– and search for– extraterrestrial life*. Hopewell, N.J.: Ecco Press.

Wickramasinghe, C. (2003). Panspermia according to Hoyle. *Astrophysics & Space Science, 285*(2), 535-538.

Wickramasinghe, C. (2011). ASTROBIOLOGY AND PANSPERMIA. *Consciências*(4), 69-74.

Williams, P. (2017). Darwin's Rottweiler & the Public Understanding of Science. *Philosophy Now,* (120). Retrieved from https://philosophynow.org/issues/44/Darwins_Rottweiler_and_the_Public_Understanding_of_Science

Woese, C. R., Kandler, O., & Wheelis, M. L. (1990). Towards a natural system of organisms: proposal for the domains Archaea, Bacteria, and Eucarya. *Proceedings of the National Academy of Sciences, 87*(12), 4576-4579. doi:10.1073/pnas.87.12.4576

Woodward, J. A., Bisbee, C. T., & Bennett, J. E. (1984). MMPI CORRELATES OF RELATIVELY LOCALIZED BRAIN DAMAGE. *Journal of Clinical Psychology, 40*(4), 961-969.

Index